Praise for *Twenty-Two*

"Allison is a good friend of mine. She knows about life and love and joy and compassion and friendship. These aren't just a collection of letters, they are a series of invitations for you to see yourself more accurately, more compassionately, and more joyfully. It's a discussion about your bright future more than what may have been a painful past. It's a long conversation with a trusted friend."

—BOB GOFF, *NEW YORK TIMES* BESTSELLING AUTHOR OF *LOVE DOES*

"Allison's wisdom and kindness shine through in every word of these letters. *Twenty-Two* is a fantastic source of encouragement and confidence for women of all ages, especially those moving through the college years."

—BETSY MILLER & DONALD MILLER, *NEW YORK TIMES* BESTSELLING AUTHOR OF *BLUE LIKE JAZZ* AND *SCARY CLOSE*

"If I could speak to the younger me, I would have nothing to say. I'd just slap her with this book."

—JEANNIE MAI, TELEVISION PERSONALITY AND STYLE EXPERT

"Young women need this book. All women need this book. With clarity, depth, and vulnerability, Allison writes an impressive tome on mentorship, faith, personal discovery, and becoming. A refreshing and much-needed perspective on womanhood that allows for all things rather than constricting the feminine to a set of expectations. I am personally grateful for this exceptional work."

—KIRSTEN HAGLUND, MISS AMERICA 2008, NATIONAL TELEVISION POLITICAL COMMENTATOR, HOST, AND WOMEN'S HEALTH ADVOCATE

"Allison is the ideal role model for girls of this generation. Her inspiration, faith-filled point of view, intellect, and wisdom shine through in this book so much so that every parent of girls should encourage their daughters to read it. Allison practices what she preaches and leads by example. She's the real deal."

—CAITLIN CROSBY BENWARD, FOUNDER AND CEO OF THE GIVING KEYS

"Plato believed that the stories the young first encounter should be models of virtue. Sadly, many modern books are empty wrappers of thought-candy that stimulate our brains but cannot sustain our hunger for substance. In the midst of such a moment, Allison Trowbridge offers a book of plummeting depth that still manages to both dazzle and captivate. *Twenty-Two* is a timeless guide to life and love, grief and celebration that lunges at you with both the spirit of Plato and flashes of uncommon wisdom. If you're a young woman—or young man, actually—you cannot afford to miss this book."

—JONATHAN MERRITT, CONTRIBUTING WRITER FOR THE *ATLANTIC* AND AUTHOR OF *LEARNING TO SPEAK GOD FROM SCRATCH*

"During the formative years of our early twenties, we search for wisdom, direction, and the heart of a trusted friend. Allison's is the voice of a familiar sister and you'll feel loved by every page."

—SARAH DUBBELDAM, EDITOR-IN-CHIEF OF *DARLING* MAGAZINE

"*Twenty-Two* is a stunning read. Page after page I found it to be insightful, hopeful, and spoken from a heart of love. I will be buying this book for my little sisters and the young women I mentor and love. I wish I had this book at twenty-two, yet it's a book that's never too late to read."

—ESTHER FLEECE, SPEAKER AND AUTHOR OF *NO MORE FAKING FINE*

"Our generation has never been in greater need of strong women to guide the conversation of female empowerment within faith communities. Trowbridge finds the balance between boldness and grace, stirring bravery within the heart of any young woman. After reading *Twenty-Two*, I'm reminded that being twenty-four is a time for trust and adventure!"

—MORIAH PETERS, RECORDING ARTIST

"I love this book! Allie's writing pulls you in, makes you part of her world with great stories and sobering truths. It's inspiring and encouraging and an invitation to live big. Allie is the friend and mentor you wish you had in college, and reading *Twenty-Two* is like a walk on the beach or an afternoon at a café with her. This book is timeless and lovely and will steal your heart. You need this!"

—KATE MERRICK, AUTHOR OF *AND STILL SHE LAUGHS*

TWENTY-TWO

Letters to a Young Woman
Searching for Meaning

ALLISON TROWBRIDGE

NELSON
BOOKS

An Imprint of Thomas Nelson

Published in Nashville, Tennessee, by Nelson Books, an imprint of Thomas Nelson. Nelson Books and Thomas Nelson are registered trademarks of HarperCollins Christian Publishing, Inc.

Published in association with Alive Literary Agency, www.aliveliterary.com.

Unless otherwise noted, all photos are from the author's personal collection.

Thomas Nelson titles may be purchased in bulk for educational, business, fundraising, or sales promotional use. For information, please e-mail SpecialMarkets@ ThomasNelson.com.

Scripture quotations are taken from the Holy Bible, New International Version®, NIV®. Copyright © 1973, 1978, 1984, 2011 by Biblica, Inc.® Used by permission of Zondervan. All rights reserved worldwide. www.zondervan.com. The "NIV" and "New International Version" are trademarks registered in the United States Patent and Trademark Office by Biblica, Inc.®

Any Internet addresses, phone numbers, or company or product information printed in this book are offered as a resource and are not intended in any way to be or to imply an endorsement by Thomas Nelson, nor does Thomas Nelson vouch for the existence, content, or services of these sites, phone numbers, companies, or products beyond the life of this book.

ISBN 978-0-7180-7811-9 (eBook)

Library of Congress Cataloging-in-Publication Data
ISBN 978-0-7180-7816-4
Names: Trowbridge, Allison, author.
Title: Twenty-two : letters to a young woman searching for meaning / Allison Trowbridge.
Description: Nashville, Tennessee : Nelson Books, [2017]
Identifiers: LCCN 2016036963 | ISBN 9780718078164
Subjects: LCSH: Conduct of life. | Young women--Psychology. | Vocational guidance. | Meaning (Philosophy) | Spiritual life.
Classification: LCC BJ1589 .T76 2017 | DDC 170.84/22--dc23 LC record available at https://lccn.loc.gov/2016036963

Printed in the United States of America

17 18 19 20 21 LSC 10 9 8 7 6 5 4 3 2 1

To every young woman
who is, or was, or ever will be Ash.
This story is yours.

And to Daisy Love,
who showed us and went before us.

CONTENTS

PART IV: Senior

INTRODUCTION

I t was late in the spring of senior year, and my world was charging toward a new upheaval: college graduation. One warm evening, the night alive with uncertainty and expectation, my roommate and I drove home and parked the car outside our apartment. We leaned the seats back to gaze at the sky and stayed there talking till dawn, dreaming about years yet to unfold and laughing over memories until our faces hurt.

As we stared into the starry abyss of our future, we wondered if we were really prepared to face all the changes that lay before us. "I wish there was a book that spoke to all the questions and pressures and hopes we have in this season of life," I sighed. "We need that kind of guidance, and nothing like it exists."

We were silent for a moment, then I added, "Maybe I'll write that book someday."

In the years after graduation, life got busy. And in the process I gained a little more of the wisdom I wished I'd had that night at twenty-two. I went on to help shape a social movement and build an anti-slavery organization, then became a partner in an impact fund, where we incubated and invested in social enterprises to generate sustainable change. I had the chance to travel across the globe and build relationships with some of the most influential leaders of today.

Through it all, my heart for young women and belief in their power to impact the world only amplified. Then one morning during a business trip in London, I awoke jet-lagged at dawn with the concept of *Twenty-Two* resounding in my mind. The book would not be a traditional compilation of advice and opinions like I'd once imagined: it would be a relationship. A relationship between the real me and a fictional character who represents

all the young women I've ever met or mentored along the way. It would be a correspondence that spoke to all the deepest life questions we almost uniformly possessed. I envisioned a friendship that would resonate with any young woman in the midst of her own journey. A journey that is, in itself, the destination.

My college graduation, when I was twenty-two.

What follows is the book conceived after my college night of dreaming. This is the book I so desperately wanted to read when I was twenty-two.

Sincerely,

Allison

PART I

FRESHMAN

CHAPTER 1

ON SEASONS & ARRIVING

Had we but world enough and time.

ANDREW MARVELL

SEPTEMBER 2

Dear Ashley,

The answer to your question is yes. A resounding, enthusiastic YES. Consider this letter the first among many. Twenty-two, to be exact.

New Beginnings

It's the second of September, and everything is changing—the pace of the streets, the weight of the air—as nature turns its colors in gold anticipation. Summer has yawned its last afternoon, our espadrilles have been traded for argyle, and everyone is walking with a briskness in their step. Fall is my favorite season. It feels like life is moving, the world is tilting, the hemisphere bowing its annual curtsy to meet the coming chill.

I think I love fall because I love new beginnings. And tweed, and ombré leaves, and those sickeningly sweet pumpkin lattes. September signals the start of something, and for you, dear girl, this month marks one of the greatest beginnings of your life.

The Westmont bagpipers. They know how to make the parents cry.

It may also be one of the most unsettling. The best of times can also bring the hardest of changes, and the high you're on now may soon dip into an aching of uncertainty and questions you can't answer yet.

I remember being where you are today: walking down that worn dirt path, through oaks and old white colonnades, bagpipes blaring sanctimoniously as a warm wind lifts the scent of kumquats and lavender, the nearby sea, and new beginnings. You feel awkward and at home all at once. It's surreal in the way that any life milestone is surreal, built up with so much anticipation before it. And then the day finally comes, and the moment arrives, and you realize you're still the same you. But everything else is different. You are still today who you were yesterday, only now the surroundings, and the people, and the tomorrows have changed.

First day of kindergarten! With my pink lunchbox.

First days are magic: invigorating, nerve-racking, and totally freeing. My memories flood back to another first day. The beginning of elementary school, walking into a classroom for the first time, shaking Mrs. Saam's hand. It was large and warm and inviting and otherworldly.

Kindergarten! I was thrilled.

As I boldly grasped my pink lunch box—my armor and social-normalizer—my mom asked, with all a mother's emotion, "Honey, how am I going to get by every day without your help?"

"Don't worry, Mommy," I comforted her. "You'll always have my help in your heart." And away I went.

It was, I think, a foreshadowing of our drive thirteen years later down the California coast, moving me to college freshman year. I fell asleep somewhere south of Santa Cruz, and my sweet mom cried the whole rest of the way. Three and a half hours. I awoke just north of Santa Barbara, so excited and nervous I didn't notice her puffy eyes.

Something tells me your momma did the same.

These transitions, Ash, are bittersweet. But you and I both know we only gain the road ahead if we leave the traveled road behind.

Seas the Day

Tell me how you're holding up this week, dear girl. How are you processing this massive life move you've embarked on?

I'm giddy with excitement for your "firsts." The first awkward meetings with lifelong friends, the first classes that will lead to majors and internships and careers. The first time you realize you're away—I mean, really away—from home. Away from all the comforts and familiarities, the soothing drudgery of predictable days, and thrust instead into the reckless, wild ride we call collegiate life. I can almost taste the cafeteria food.

I envy this new adventure you're stepping into. I envy it in the way I would envy a friend setting off to sail the Pacific. I know there will be sea-green days of sickness, ink-black nights of storms, and salt-encrusted everything. There will be exhaustion and disorientation and loss, and so much open ocean you could go blind from all the blue. But I envy that what's staring you straight in the face is nothing but that open ocean. The setting that will bring your miseries will also carry new worlds of delight: the bronze sun above, the wind whipping your hair, adventure stowed like treasure beneath your mainsail. Nothing but you and your boat and the possibility of a sea that will shape you and teach you ten thousand things you never knew about yourself, and would never have known, had you not left the comfort of the familiar wood dock.

Change is fraught with uncertainty and fear. But it's an exhilarating fear, don't you think? You feel as though your life is unfolding before you and every offer is available. Every failure and triumph and heartbreak and victory lap a pending possibility.

Which leads to my confession.

The Journey

Ash, for as long as I can remember, I've had a deep-seated sense that one day I was going to arrive—that I would wake up one morning and stretch out my arms to the world and revel in a sense of finished self. Probably around the age of thirty-five.

Have you felt this?

I never used to admit it to myself, and I certainly didn't announce it to anyone else. What normal teenage girl daydreams about her graduation into midthirties adulthood? I'm almost embarrassed to write it now. And yet, from a very young age, I had this unrelenting sense I was moving toward a destination. I was becoming someone, becoming the finished me, and one day I was going to get there. Even as a child, I couldn't wait to meet this worldly, wisdom-filled, thirty-five-year-old self.

I'll never forget the evening that all changed.

I was just a few years older than you are now, lying stomach-down on my mattress on the floor. We were approaching the start of senior year, and my girlfriends and I had moved four miles off campus into the Country Club Apartments. Each night we piled side by side into rooms that smelled like chipping paint and aging carpet, with more telephone wire than country club in our view, and it felt like the ultimate freedom.

I remember that evening so well: bright clangs of laughter and dinner dishes in the other room, the final strokes of neon sky outside my screen door. The flimsy lamp that had followed us since freshman year burned amber overhead as I flipped through a wine-red devotional: Oswald Chambers's classic, *My Utmost for His Highest*.

I've always equated underlining to learning, so, pen poised, I found the day's page: July 28. I skimmed the first paragraph and, out of habit, pressed a line of ink beneath what seemed an important stretch of words: "What we see as only the process of reaching a particular end . . ."

I stopped. I put my pen down. I read the passage again.

> We should never have the thought that our dreams of success are God's purpose for us. In fact, His purpose may be exactly the opposite. We have the idea that God is leading us toward a particular end or a desired goal, but He is not. The question of whether or not we arrive at a particular goal is of little importance, and reaching it becomes merely an episode along the way. What we see as only the process of reaching a particular end, God sees as the goal itself.[1]

Ash, the soul—tuned by character—is an instrument. When words strike a chord, our spirit resonates. I think the heart can discern a cadence of truth as much as the ear can discern a melody, and that night, those words felt like music.

I lay there for a while, on my mind's empty beach, as the cold truths caught me up like a tide. What we see as the journey, God sees as the destination. I wondered if I'd had life a bit wrong all these years.

Once upon a time, I believed that who I was today didn't matter as much as who I would become. That what mattered most was whether I achieved the goals I set for myself, the goals I felt called to. I believed that hitting the sands of some tropical shore was what made the sailing trip worthwhile. But God wasn't waiting for me to get somewhere. He saw my life, the entire span of it, from birth to death, all at once. And he loved me as I was and as I am and also as I would be, in some eternal moment outside of time.

I'm not sure where you are with God, but I'd love to know. I have a lot more to learn about you, Ash, and you about me, as well. But what I do know is this: That night was a revelation for me. The thought washed over me like a wave, and I pressed in until I was soaked. Absorbed by, and absorbing, this new reality: our life's journey is our life's destination.

Be Everything

We are living in one of the most remarkable periods in history for young women. When I look at you, dear girl, I see limitless opportunity. Never have young women been given greater access to the world—education to seize, information to gain, platforms to create, blogs to post, social networks to join, online stores to shop!

Think about this, Ash: With just a credit card and a travel-booking site, you can be anywhere on the globe within seventy-two hours, reading the comment thread on your Insta-posts before you even feel jet-lagged. Your dad might not be thrilled with your reckless spontaneity—but that's not the point.

When in history has this level of access existed for an eighteen-year-old, let alone a woman?

A young woman, especially in the West, has never had more choices before her than the girl of today. Ours is the era of options and opportunities, and endless public opinions on how we might make the most of them. And yet, the girls I see exiting our twenty-first-century graduating classes seem burdened with more questions than answers, more pressure than prospects, and more feelings of doubt than direction.

I think our generation is caving under the many new and, dare I say, unrealistic pressures of this brave new world: the societal, social, familial, and, most of all, personal expectations for what we should make of this life.

There's pressure to meet your dream guy, to land the perfect job, to design a storybook home, to raise a small tribe of cherubic children. Pressure to look like the cover girls, to know the most glamorous people, to attract millions of followers, and, of course, to change the world. Or at least end extreme poverty by the time you hit thirty. I hope you don't feel all these pressures yet, but you probably will. I certainly feel them, and more.

A woman named Courtney E. Martin once wrote, "We are the daughters of feminists who said 'You can be anything' and we heard 'You have to be everything.'"[2]

Don't be everything, Ash. Be you.

Don't do everything. Do you.

There's only one you, and the world needs you desperately.

Onward

I'm so glad I saw you last week, dear girl. You have courage and character and a beauty that breathes deep. I'm honored you would ask me to walk with you over what could be the most transformative season of your life.

It certainly was in mine.

I've never been terrific at keeping in touch, and the coming distance won't help, but I promise you this: I will write you every other month over these precious college years. Please write to me the months in between, so I can know you better and know how you are. Tell me about all of the challenges, joys, and triumphs of everyday living, for living is truly a triumph.

I can't give you all the answers, but I hope I can help you ask some good questions. I think asking, the very act of it, is our lifeblood. Wonder and courage pump through us as we question, giving breath to our beings, strength to our bones. Some days it's tempting to live in concrete planes of black and white, but the world is full of color, and growing up is learning how to navigate the hues and the infinite gradients of grey.

There's so much more to say: on romance and justice, on wanderlust and red lipstick, and on the goal itself. I'm excited for this season you're stepping into, Ash. Thank you for letting me journey with you.

Always,

X

PS—Do you mind that I call you Ash? It suits you.
PPS—Call your mom.

> What we call the beginning is often the end
> And to make an end is to make a beginning.
> The end is where we start from.
>
> *T. S. ELIOT*

CHAPTER 2

ON BEAUTY & SEEING

Everything has beauty but not everyone sees it.
CONFUCIUS

NOVEMBER 2

Ash,

My dear college student, I don't know where to begin! I have so many questions.

How do you like your classes? Are you enjoying the day-to-day? Have you fallen in love with this glittery seaside city? Or plain-old fallen in love? I can't believe just as you are settling in, I am preparing to move away—to San Francisco of all places. But I know you are exactly where you're supposed to be, and I am too. I think.

Sunset Decisions

Thank you for your letter, Ash. I cherished every word.

You wrote about the peace you felt the moment you first stepped onto campus, and I remember feeling the same. Which

First campus visit when I made my mind up. I was going to Westmont.

was strange, because until that point I'd been convinced I would attend some legendary East Coast school with more college students than the population of the town where I grew up. I wanted to spread my wings, and I assumed that meant getting as far away from the California coast as I could.

Then I set foot onto Westmont.

I was in the midst of college applications, and my parents thought it would be a good idea to drive down the coast and let me see a few schools before I made a decision. You know, get a sense for what the next four years could look like, since I really had nothing to picture. They had never sent a kid to college, and I had never been, so the process was new for all of us.

The first place we stopped was a state school, which looked exciting, except several students from my high school were headed there and I've always had a strange desire to be different. *Check that one off the list.* Next we stopped at my dad's alma mater, which was large and vibrant and stunning. *This could be an option*, I thought. Until my dad, with the enthusiasm of a first-time campus tour guide, proceeded to show us the student housing and proudly pointed out all the places he'd lived with flea infestations. He drove us past buildings that were set on fire during campus protests in the 1970s, and told stories of the wild audiences who attended the rock shows he played with his band. My mom shook her head slowly in the front seat as Dad relived the good ol' days and didn't understand my lack of zeal about the school. I'm sure the fleas have long since migrated south—not least because of the fires—but my mind was made up. *Sorry, Dad.*

The clouds rolled in as our journey continued, and I wondered if any college would be right for me. We drove south down the coast and pulled into a small 1930s estate-converted-to-campus tucked amid the sycamores of Montecito. I had seen Westmont's booth at college fairs and felt an instant draw to the scenic shots and smiling faces on the display boards. It looked magical . . . too magical. Too lovely for the stoic hardship I was certain college life would entail. Plus, it was small and on the West Coast, which did not fit my vision of getting lost in a sea of twenty thousand preppy people. But then we parked, and I walked along Kerrwood Lawn, and something in me changed.

Sometimes things that make the most sense in life don't make logical sense in our minds, at first. They are heart-knowing, not head-knowing. It was early January—winter break. The campus was foggy and cold and empty. There was nothing alluring, nothing that matched the sunny, palm tree landscapes on the pamphlets, but Westmont felt like coming home. I can't describe it any other way.

We spent an hour there, strolling the quiet hills, and I took the place in. As we drove off that evening along the ocean-lined 101, I turned back and saw the sky lit up in a brilliant flame of color, blurring with intensity like an oversaturated photo. I'd never seen a sunset like that before. My parents made plans in the front of the car and my brother nodded along to the music in his headphones, but the moment, for me, was spiritual. After that evening, I didn't worry about the college admissions process or fuss over the other applications that had once caused so much stress. That sunset had secured my fate.

I knew, that I knew, that I knew—I was going to Westmont.

Major Choices

Now Ash, let's discuss the overwhelming question hanging over your head—the great decision that will direct the course of your next four years. The choice that could set the bearing of your life's career, determine the places you go and the people you meet, shape the human being you become, and potentially decide the plot of land where you are buried.

Your major.

I began college with a plan to study religion. Yes, I know what you're thinking: I'm even more saintly than you thought. But I actually chose religious studies because I loved my church youth group and my leader and mentor, Lindsey, and I wanted to be like her. I'm loads of fun at summer camp and thought if I majored in religion then someone might hire me as a youth group leader.

This pious plan lasted a full three weeks and one welcome barbeque before I acquired a wandering eye. Oh, the wily temptations of greener academic fields. I heard a senior talk about her decision to be a communication studies major, and I envied the blissful, well-branded classes she must be attending. That was my gateway sin, in a collegiate sense. Once I opened my mind to majors beyond religious studies, every discipline became enticing.

I love liberal arts colleges because they require you to sample every dish at the banquet table of knowledge, and I had a smorgasbord. I devoured courses in history and doctrine and literature. I enjoyed them each in different ways, which led to an increasing uncertainty about what track my life was supposed to take. I had wanted to go to law school for as long as I could remember and thought I should pursue political science, and probably philosophy, to boost my future LSAT scores.

Then again, I also wanted to speak another language to charm future suitors, so maybe a minor in French. Although, English could be ideal, because writing was key to a law career, and a background in history would strengthen my future run for president. Or art history, perhaps. My mom was an art teacher, and my family owned an art store, so this plan made a lot of sense. Also, Prince William was an art history major, so I thought that would give us something to talk about if he ever came calling. At least, that's what I thought until I met the business students. I'd never even thought about studying business! It seemed they knew something about the way the world operated that the rest of us did not, and there weren't many women in the business department, which implied a challenge. I love a good challenge. I would have to explore business as well.

I toyed with the idea of majoring in a liberal arts education. Can people do that?

Finally, one long year of exploring later, I settled on communication studies, the canon of coursework I'd initially longed for but had not allowed myself to entertain. I figured I could always pursue French or philosophy as a hobby, but if I didn't learn how to communicate well, I wouldn't be much good at anything entrepreneurial. I might have an idea for a company that could reshape the modern world, but if I couldn't communicate the concept clearly, I would never impact anyone. The fact is, I had mostly ruled out communication studies because it sounded like *fun*. But who's to say we can't enjoy the way we spend our days?

I had tried in vain to plan my perfect future, Ash, pointing every area of focus toward some ephemeral haze of a career or grad school application or life plan. Until, finally, I gave up— and just decided to study what I loved.

What to Do

And so, my dear, I suppose that's the advice I have for you, even though it's as unoriginal as telling you to eat your fruits and vegetables and get eight hours of sleep at night. Which you should also be doing!

Study what you love.

Devote yourself to a topic you want to think about, write about, and read books about, regardless of whether or not they're assigned.

You aren't here to memorize information, my love—although it might feel that way before midterms. You are here to get a liberal arts education, so you can learn how to *learn*. To become a lifelong learner, as our college president, Dr. Gaede, used to say. You aren't in trade school; you are learning the trade of learning. This skill will prepare you most for whatever vocation life throws at you.

Ash, this time in college will help you hone the skills that make you unique. As you learn about the world's greatest needs, you'll begin to see where you, with all your gifts, quirks, passions, and even shortcomings, can rise to meet those needs in a thousand meaningful ways. It's not your job to save the world, but it is your calling to offer your best to it. More than anything, that means learning to serve, and to listen, and to love others well.

It's also worth reminding you that finding your life's work is an ever-evolving process. I never knew this starting out. I imagined careers were like airplanes, and universities the airports where we chose a destination before making our way to the corresponding gate. Careers and colleges may have looked that way in decades past, but not so in our present age.

A vocation today is more often like a road trip, with no set course or destination. All you have are the combined limits and opportunities of the car you are driving, the gas in your tank, and the many roads unrolling before you that will lead to innumerable places exciting and new. Of course, you may end up taking a roundabout course to get somewhere, but what makes the road trip worthwhile may be the very time spent on the scenic route. So ease off the gas pedal a bit and take some time to choose your soundtrack. Stop for photos at the lookouts.

What makes you light up inside, Ash? Pursue that field, and study it with abandon. The future will work itself out, in time.

As Children

You asked about my favorite teachers through the years, and I've since remembered one more who made the most unlikely, yet maybe the greatest, impact on me.

My ceramics teacher in high school, Mr. Emery.

My mom is an art teacher and could have taught me the craft on her potter's wheel in our garage, but I drank in the life lessons I learned in the course and kept signing up. Mr. Emery's classes were half ceramics and half philosophy, if you really broke them down. I made vases and teapots and giant glazed serving bowls, and then I would stay after-hours debating the finer points of religion and spirituality and the meaning of life—having, as I did, most of life figured out by sixteen. He would talk about his perspectives on the world and his pilgrimages in the desert and would challenge the very basis of my opinions and beliefs. I was a young and overzealous teen, but he engaged with me like I was the most important meeting he'd had all week.

At first I thought Mr. Emery was out there, and then I thought he was brilliant, and then I just appreciated him whether I agreed with him or not. He didn't believe in Christianity as I did, but he liked the idea of Jesus and gave me C. S. Lewis books to read as homework. These books—*The Great Divorce* and *Till We Have Faces*—still impact me to this day.

One of my favorite things Mr. Emery did happened at the beginning of each semester. We would walk into class and there on the otherwise empty wall would be a picture taken decades ago of an adorable, bright-eyed child. He would instruct each of us to bring in a picture of ourselves as a toddler, and by the next week the back wall would be covered with our childhood photos. All of them surrounded that first picture, which—we would discover—was of him.

"When you are tempted to be angry or frustrated or unforgiving toward one another," he would say, "or toward me when you receive your grades, I want you to look at these photos and see each of us as we once were—as children."

The class of teens would fall silent. "It's impossible to show anything but compassion toward a toddler," he'd continue. "If you begin to see the child in each of the schoolmates around you today, tomorrow you may see the child in everyone. A child who is vulnerable, and learning, and lovable, and loved."

Imagine, dear Ash, how many wars would wane if we saw one another as children.

I want to challenge you to do something. Yes, I realize I'm sounding mentor-ly now. I challenge you, Ash, to see people. I mean, to *really* see people. Not with your eyes, but with your heart.

Most of us are afraid of being seen.

We are often so afraid of how we look, how we talk, what we'll say, and what we won't say, that we soothe ourselves in our fear by casting a critical eye toward others. We see what the world sees, and we make assumptions. But I know, to a small degree, the depths of your character, Ash, and I know you're capable of seeing past the surface things.

When you meet new people throughout your time on campus, don't judge their shoes, their faces, their social standings. When you start to glance at their outfits, try instead to get a glimpse of their hearts. Picture them as the children they once were. Imagine their hopes and their fears and their dreams, and you'll be so full of love for them you won't remember to worry about yourself.

Body Talk

Speaking of how we see others, let's talk for a moment about how we see ourselves. I've been thinking about that phone conversation we had last week and a few of the comments you made. It's okay to not be crazy about your appearance sometimes, Ash, but I want you to dig deeper into why you're so hard on yourself. I want to encourage you to give yourself some grace. It breaks my heart to see how much we all struggle with the ways we see our physical selves. I wonder if it's not the greatest burden for women in our culture's comparison age.

But I get it. I mean, I *really* get it. I feel the pain and pressure too.

I love my body, and I resent my body, all at once. It's the border between my soul and the world; it keeps me both protected and trapped. It defines me, confines me; it empowers me, devours me; it has limits, it breaks down. It allows me to dance in the redwoods and to jump into waves and to paint. My mind cannot control or shape my body's natural form. It grows and ages outside my command, programmed by some preordered DNA that nothing can override. And yet, it's mine—and no one else's. It's the only one I've got and the only one I'll ever have. This side of heaven, at least.

There's a universal "no returns" policy on bodies, as much

as I'd love to go shopping and swapping mine some days. And no argument with God will ever warrant a trade, no matter how much I fuss or complain, sweet-talk or explain. No exchanges, no returns.

I can't take my body back, but I can tend to it. My mind is a gardener to this wild, messy, beautiful plot of land we call our being. I can feed it and care for it and even decorate it. And that's really half the fun: the decoration. But so many young women, myself included, focus too much energy on trying to look like someone else, when all we can and should be is the healthiest, most vibrant versions of the physical selves we've been given. Besides, regardless of how we see ourselves, the standard of beauty our grandchildren know will be different from today's cultural ideal.

Believe it or not, some days I'm grateful I don't have a perfect body. I'm serious! Because then I would have to worry about losing its perfection someday. As it is, I'm not so enamored with what I've got, so I don't suppose I'll feel a devastating loss when it all starts to sag. Life is harder when you base your worth on your appearance, for it will always, eventually, let you down. Like any living thing, we cannot be preserved. It's not our body's nature. My darling, there is neither a beauty on this planet that won't wither with age nor a flower given to bloom that will not wilt and fade.

I've heard it said that only the perishable can be beautiful, which is why we are unmoved by artificial flowers.

I suppose that's part of the wonder of bodies: their absolute, undeniable frailty. One day they will up and quit, and there's nothing we can do when that final moment comes. We can spend our whole lives running from a certain end, or we can welcome it. For the promise of an end is the very thing that proves we are alive.

Merely Decorative

Have you seen the movie *Little Women*, based on the nineteenth-century classic by Louisa May Alcott? I watch it every autumn, without fail, and reminisce over make-believing childhood days spent in the South with my cousins, Rebekah, Rachel, and Ruth. The mother in *Little Women*, Marmee, reminds me so much of my Auntie Fawn, who recently passed away from cancer.

In one of my favorite scenes, Marmee cradles her eldest daughter, Meg, on her bed. Meg has just returned from a ball where she's tried to impress the popular girls and potential suitors by wearing a revealing gown, drinking excessively, and acting in a way that doesn't match her deeper values. After collapsing at home in discouragement, Meg admits that she liked her moment of attention, despite the subsequent sense of self-loathing.

"I only care what you think of yourself," Marmee says. "If you feel your value lies in being merely decorative, I fear that someday you might find yourself believing that's all that you really are."

What is beauty to you, Ash? Is it found in being merely decorative, or is it something more? Is it a cultural ideal, or is it a greater ideal deep inside you?

You know, I have plenty of girlfriends who have modeled through the years, and several who've won the most prestigious beauty pageants in the world. Yet it seems to me the more they are celebrated for their appearances, the more they are also torn apart for their imperfections. The more they achieve some elusive ideal, the more comment threads debate their flaws. I have friends who've been sent home from modeling jobs because their faces were too puffy or were told they needed plastic surgery to "make it" in the modeling world. They were criticized and judged in ways that would impact the self-worth of even the most confident girl.

One precious friend won a major beauty pageant a few years back, and I asked her what it felt like in the first weeks afterward. Was it a high? Was she in shock? Total bliss?

"I went on antidepressants," she said.

The higher you climb, the more people will stand by waiting to tear you down. "I've never felt uglier than when I won Miss America," another told me. At the end of the day, I know each of these friends would agree: being externally beautiful does not make you internally happy. It is a wonderful gift to have beauty, dear Ash, but its fleeting expression ought never be our aim. The older I get, the more I'm convinced that what we all desire most is to feel comfortable in our own skin. To be confident just being who we are.

As Marmee went on to say, "Time erodes all such beauty, but what it cannot diminish is the wonderful workings of your mind. Your humor, your kindness, and your moral courage. These are the things I cherish so in you."

External beauty is just the icing on the character of your life. People may be enticed by icing, but no one wants to eat a whole cake of it. So be countercultural, Ash. Be a woman who's willing to step into a purpose that's bigger than being merely decorative.

The world is waiting for you.

Much Is Given

One chilly November morning during my freshman year, I was listening to Dr. Shirley Mullen, the school's provost, teach our history course. Tall and lean with a crown of red hair, she was brilliant and commanding and noble. That morning she detoured from the content outlined on the syllabus, as great professors typically do, and I'll never forget what she said: "To whom much is given, much is required."

I'd heard this phrase my whole life from my parents. It'd become a mantra of sorts for me, but I never knew it was a verse in the Bible.

"From everyone who has been given much, much will be demanded," Dr. Mullen scribbled on the board, "and from the one who has been entrusted with much, much more will be asked." [1]

As the minute hand stretched to signal the end of class, Dr. Mullen gave an impassioned appeal about the rarity of our education, the privilege we have to scan the annals of history and impact our world. Never before has humanity known more, and never have we had a greater responsibility to do something worthy of this wealth of information and opportunities.

"If we knew, if we could truly grasp the reality of what we have and the responsibility it affords us," she exclaimed, "it would keep us up at night."

Did this keep me up at night? *Sometimes*, I thought. *Probably not often enough.*

I left shaken, inspired, and grateful I didn't understand my full responsibility to the world yet. I'll never forget that morning because Dr. Mullen's passionate speech shifted the paradigm of my taken-for-granted education. And I did toss and turn for a number of nights after that.

We have so much life to live, Ash, and so few breaths to do it in.

Yours,

x

PS—How are you and your little sister getting along? Better, I hope?

Nature's first green is gold,
Her hardest hue to hold.

Her early leaf's a flower;
But only so an hour.
Then leaf subsides to leaf.
So Eden sank to grief,
So dawn goes down to day.
Nothing gold can stay.

ROBERT FROST

CHAPTER 3

ON TIME & BECOMING

> We have what we seek,
> it is there all the time, and if we give it time,
> it will make itself known to us.
>
> *THOMAS MERTON*

JANUARY 7

Dearest Ash,

Happy New Year!

There's such energy in this week. Do you feel it, dear girl? A light humming all around as the world reflects and rests and prepares to break into something new. Resolutions have been made, and practiced, and—if they're like mine—forgotten already.

A new year marks the passage of time for all of us. As we hang our calendars we realize how much we have grown through the tiniest of increments, as the compound result of slight daily change is brought suddenly into sharp focus. New years are like tree houses we climb into for an afternoon to look out across the vista of forest we've been wandering through, a place we pause to chart our course.

New years give new perspective.

Becoming Real

So far this year I haven't done much resolution making, but I have done a lot of reflecting. How about you, darling girl?

I'll be one year older on the twenty-second this month, and in spite of a culture bent on immortal youth, I've realized something true to the contrary. Life isn't so much about growing up or growing old as it is about *becoming real*. Think of the Tin Man, who journeyed all the way to the Emerald City in search of a heart—only to discover the gift he longed for already beat inside his chest. What he'd gained, it turned out, was not a physical heart but the capacity to love along the way. He was, in a sense, becoming real.

When I was a year old, my godparents gave me a white stuffed bunny with floppy legs and round black eyes and two pink stitches that crisscrossed for her mouth. She was an Easter gift from a local department store, and since I was too young to have any say in the matter, my mom named her Esther because it sounded like the holiday. There was nothing remarkable or even memorable about my bunny, but to me, she was perfect. And she became more perfect the more I loved her. The more I kissed her forehead and dressed her in my baby clothes and wore away her fur until raw material showed through, the more she became *Esther*.

Loving my bunny, Esther.

There's a beautiful passage in a classic children's book about another beloved bunny of this kind—the Velveteen Rabbit.

> You become. It takes a long time. That's why it doesn't happen often to people who break easily, or have sharp edges, or who have to be carefully kept. Generally, by the time you are Real, most of your hair has been loved off, and your eyes drop out and you get loose in the joints and very shabby. But these things don't matter at all, because once you are Real you can't be ugly, except to people who don't understand.[1]

Our world doesn't talk much about becoming real, Ash. It talks about youth and beauty and amassing wealth and influence. But our culture has it wrong. Life is not about becoming somebody; life is about the process of becoming.

Becoming real is the reason you and I are here.

The Red Mailbox

When I think about becoming real, I think of Marge. Beloved Marge: the woman who has shared her home and her life with me for the past year and a half.

You can't miss the house on Hot Springs Road, its iconic red mailbox welcoming passersby. If you head down the lane beneath the California pepper leaves, past the towering eucalyptus, you'll be greeted by a single olive tree, her brown ranch house reclining behind it. The place is elegant yet understated— Marge was never one for show. Except for the yard, which is always blooming with a hundred different hues, full of primrose and hydrangeas and poppies beneath the ancient oaks. Winter at Marge's house tastes like fresh figs and artichokes; it smells like warm persimmon and garden rose and cool, damp earth.

It's a place where I've watched generations of young and old pass through for an afternoon tea or a walk in the garden or to drop off a holiday gift. I felt special, getting to live with Marge. But the fact is, I am just *one* in a long line of people Marge and her late husband, Hugh, invited to take shelter for a season in their Montecito home. My friend Christina resided there for two years before me, and to this day we call ourselves de facto cousins. Marge has become a grandmother to us both.

In a word, she is golden, and it's not just the halo of honey-colored hair that encircles her head. Marge's glow is soul deep, in the way a coin at the bottom of a pool makes the surface shimmer with light. She is as regal as the Queen of England and as warm as Belle, her old yellow Lab.

Marge has had a more profound impact on my life than almost anyone else. She has grit and quiet charisma, and she tells it like it is. I mean, *really* tells it like it is. If she doesn't like the new fella you're dating, she'll let you know it the moment he walks out the door. This became my secret means of vetting potential suitors for my friends and myself. I'd just ask if she liked the poor bloke once he left, and that would determine it.

With my mentor, Marge, at my going-away party, before I moved to San Francisco.

Katee Grace Clay

Marge was never wrong.

She also forgets she is in her mideighties. We were having lunch recently at the Montecito Inn, eating slices of their iconic coconut cake with the flair of Marie Antoinette, when a group of octogenarians pushed their walkers by.

"Look at all the *old* people in here!" Marge exclaimed. I couldn't tell if she was serious—she was likely a few years their senior.

Living with Marge has made me think about life backward, with the end in mind. I suppose she has shown me what it means to build a legacy. Marge makes me want to live out stories I can tell my grandchildren or the young people yet to be born that I'll get to mentor someday. Stories of skydiving and mountain hikes, of deep-sea dives and life-changing conversations. Stories that mean something, unlike the things I spend most of my hours worrying about—like whether I want my coffee hot or iced or when a dress will go on sale or how many likes my social media post received.

Our culture fears old age, Ash, but watching Marge has helped me embrace it. To see it like a lifetime achievement award. I want the sort of heritage she's left, to make the kind of impact she's made, one person and one community at a time.

For decades Marge and Hugh have owned an outdoor plaza in downtown Santa Barbara called La Arcada. Ivy clings to the walls of local shops framed by red tile roofs as flags from every country flutter above statues of everyday people that speckle the walkways and park benches. Those charming statues have become a local attraction over the years as tourists pause to take pictures with them. But there are no statues of Marge—here or anywhere else in the world, because her legacy has been her imprint on souls.

And that's just the way she would want it to be.

Desert Time

During the first summer I lived with Marge, I took an incredible journey: to Jordan, in the middle of the Middle East. I brought my mom—her first trip outside North America. None of that typical Paris or London first-time-traveler stuff. We went to visit my cousins who were living in Amman, the capital of the country.

"*Ahlan wha salan, fil* Jordan!" exclaimed my cousin's four-year-old twins. *Welcome to Jordan!*

I surprised myself with how comfortable I felt in the Middle East, even amid unexpected discomforts. The night we arrived I collapsed, jet-lagged and delusional, on a small bed in the guest room. Then I shot upright at five a.m., as the blaring of an Arabic chant reverberated through an open window overhead. After a few deep breaths and a laugh with my mom in the adjacent bed, I lay down once more, the Muslim call to prayer still echoing in my dreams.

We explored that buzzing Middle Eastern country with its natural wonders and ruins and then went camping in Wadi Rum. *Wadi* means "valley" in Arabic, and Jordan is known for its majestic valleys. Growing up, I hated camping. It usually involved bugs, dull days at tourist campsites, and my brother pinching my arm during hikes when my parents weren't looking. But camping in Wadi Rum was different. It was mystical.

We were greeted by a lanky, young Bedouin with an awkward smile and an epic unibrow. He loaded us onto makeshift benches in the back of a covered white pickup truck and bounced us across the amber desert. Up and down the rolling sand dunes we drove, all of them radiant shades of sepia and rose gold and burnt orange, the sky a cloudless, cornflower blue above. He showed us where Lawrence of Arabia camped, and parked atop the tallest dunes to let us run down the sides. If you run fast enough, Ash, you feel weightless, floating down the face of glittering sand.

At one point, our Bedouin friend abruptly stopped the truck and told us to get out. We did so without thinking, leaving our bags and packs in the back. "Meet me ahead!" he yelled, then sped off without us.

For a moment, I panicked. We had no belongings, no cell service, no nothing. And then I smiled, shoulders relaxing, as I drank in the moment. Conversations quieted, and we let the magnitude of space consume us.

It was a moment when time dissolved.

We followed his wheel tracks through the open desert, our spirits radiating in silence, until we rounded the corner of a glowing rock face and heard the faint undulations of Arabic music ahead. There was our guide, sitting by a small fire, *shisha* pipe in hand.

"Who wants to try first?" He grinned.

"I do!" my mom said, running forward.

Chronos Time

Until that moment in the desert, my world had been spinning, phone ringing, emails pinging, on what the Greeks called *chronos* time—time that's quantifiable, measurable, dependable, and immutable. Not even my away message could protect me from this barrage, for I willingly gave in to every whirring demand. I could not disconnect.

But then I was dropped in the desert, and I saw the world a different way. I watched the sun go down that night and rise the next morning, suspending the infinite desert in the warmth of its flame. I sipped sugared mint tea and sat in silence and let the stillness seep in.

Our world and our days run on chronos time, the time of alarm clocks and flight schedules. To be honest, I've never gotten along well with chronos. You could say we had a working relationship, but I wouldn't call us friends.

For me, chronos is a bad assembly-line manager who will crank up the conveyer belt every chance it gets. Give me a task and we'll pack it in, which is great for doing lots of things, but terrible for doing them well. I'm optimistic by nature, which makes me overoptimistic about how long things take. Maybe this is why I am five minutes late to e-v-e-r-y-thing. *Sorry about last Tuesday.* There are only a select few people this works well with, like my best friend, Christie, because we usually both show up late to meet each other, at the same time.

Elizabeth Taylor wrestled with chronos too, you know. She used to say she'd be late for her own funeral, and so, when she did pass away, they started the ceremony five minutes after the hour.

Kairos Time

As much as I wrestle with chronos time, my life has a tendency to get lost in it. Amid my constant need to achieve, I surrender my days to the clock. I strive and push and struggle and schedule and rush. But there's another kind of time the Greeks wrote about, Ash.

The time the desert taught me: *kairos.*

Kairos time is measured by moments, not minutes. It's the feeling when you watch the waves ceaselessly hit the shore or see someone you love after being a very long distance apart. Kairos is living, kinetic, moving, breathing, and expanding. If chronos clocks, then kairos creates. It's in chronos that a landscaper bills his hours working on the yard. It's in kairos that a toddler explores the infinite world of a flower patch.

Madeleine L'Engle, one of my favorite authors growing up, wrote more profoundly on time than anyone I've encountered. Her novels dealt with faith and quantum physics and things so insightful and true that she had to write the books for children. It was, she would say, too complicated for adults to understand. She described kairos as: "Real time. God's time. That time which breaks through chronos with a shock of joy."[2]

We cannot stop the physicality of time, but we can expand the space within it.

No matter what I do or buy or where I go this spring, in six months the world will turn golden, and in sixty years we will have wrinkles. But in those years, however many we're given, we have the chance to magnify the quality of days. To win wrinkles that make us more beautiful, more real, because they're made of smile lines from decades of joy ground in. The sort of wrinkles that display an authenticity and wisdom only a weathered face can possess.

In chronos, we age. In kairos, we become real. Like the Velveteen Rabbit. I don't know about you, Ash, but I want a life of kairos days.

Places

I went for a walk today along Butterfly Beach, my favorite place to stroll. The sand there is held back by a retaining wall of cement and stone, aptly named the Biltmore Wall after the glamorous hotel that reclines behind it like a Hollywood starlet.

The Biltmore Wall has a reputation among college students for a certain purpose. At Westmont we called them "DTRs," or "Define the Relationship" talks, and we always had them at the wall. We'd stare out at the endless black pool of ocean, perched on the rippling ledge of cement with our legs dangling over the side. Two souls embracing the air together, a breath away, a world apart. Getting together. Breaking up.

As I grew older, though, the wall's meaning began to change, and it became its own kind of home for me. I would return there frequently, sometimes daily, to run Belle along the loop of local road. Or I would speed down the hill from Marge's house and park my car there at dusk, catching the last bit of sunset beside other onlookers, like spectators at a fireworks display.

Ash, there are places we encounter in life that touch a certain part of us. Holy places. Locations that capture kairos and make our spinning lives stand still. These are places that speak to us. Every time we walk that street, or stand in that meadow, or stare at that shore, there it is. A sense of meaning, a stilling presence, an inexplicable peace.

For me, these places are as everyday as the areas that grew me up, and as exotic as the faraway, foreign landscapes that imprinted themselves in my memory. Each one distinct, knit as a thread in my story.

It's the hill above my parents' house that I climb after jogs. The place where I can stare down, sweaty and breathless, at my old high school and small town by the sea and process all the hard and confusing and beautiful things of growing up. It's my cousins' room in Atlanta, at the top of their creaky staircase, on the floor where I spent teenage summers writing in journals and staying up to all hours of the night musing about God, and cute boys, and the meaning of life.

It's the chapel at Westmont, and the forest in Brussels. It's a square I stumbled onto in London at dusk, where you can buy fish and chips with mushy peas. It's an expat café in Cambodia with the best caipirinhas in the world, and Ta Prohm, a playground of ruins tangled in tree roots I climbed through in a downpour. It's the hidden benches of Central Park in fall, and an overgrown trail off the Blue Ridge Parkway in Asheville. In

San Francisco, it's the chandeliered hall of the Palace Hotel and the striking columns of the Palace of Fine Arts. It's the winding cliffs leading up to Half Moon Bay through the haze and pumpkin fields and moss-covered trees. It's the waterways of Bosnia at dusk, and those copper hills of Wadi Rum when sunrise breaks across the desert and lights the world on fire.

All these places are more than destinations, or even memories, for me. They are the locations where my soul feels open to the world, centered in time and space. They are homes for my spirit, where something in me comes awake. There's a frequency I pick up here that I don't tune into otherwise. I not only speak to God in these places, I listen. I stand on hallowed ground.

The Cemetery

As I get ready to move, I've been reflecting on my years in Santa Barbara, a season that meant more to me than any other because throughout it I became more me. More real, you could say.

If I were a city, I would be Santa Barbara. It's small yet sweeping, peaceful yet vibrant, and it's built on community. People come from all over the world to pass the brilliant springs and foggy Junes and sweet Septembers here. They come to walk on the pier and lie on the beaches and dance in the streets and crack confetti eggs during August's Fiesta. But the tourists don't visit one of my favorite places in the city. I suppose few locals do either.

The Santa Barbara Cemetery. I love this city's graveyard.

It might sound macabre, but I find it inspiring. Especially as we begin a new year, as I pause to stare back at my life. You would never know it's there, tucked up on the cliffs overlooking the water. In college I would go to the cemetery some early mornings, vanilla tea latte in hand, and walk through the names put to rest in the grass and imagine their stories. I would look at the water from between the headstones and envision where my life would lead, what my stone would say.

New York Times columnist David Brooks writes often about the difference between résumé and obituary virtues—between the accomplishments we pitch potential employers and the victories and values spoken over us at our memorials.

I suppose that's why I liked visiting the cemetery, Ash. Amid the stressful absurdities of term papers and boys who didn't call, it gave me perspective. It allowed me, like my time with Marge, to look at life backward. With the end in mind.

Resolutions

I've been thinking as I write this letter that I do have a New Year's resolution, actually, and that is to let go. Whether it's painting, or writing, or cleaning, or dancing—most of the time I so desperately want to be perfect that I waste my time away with striving.

I'm resolving this year to paint in wide strokes, to write in mad flurries, to clean with broad sweeps, to dance with abandon. At least by myself. To create space for desert moments.

Let us always remember, Ash, that the goal is not to live, but to live fully alive. In the words of Emily Dickinson, "Forever—is composed of Nows."[3]

And speaking of now: I need to have you over to Marge's house soon for dinner, before I move. Why don't you bring your roommate, Madison? She sounds wonderful, and I can't wait to meet her. Let's do it on Friday, because there's such happiness to Fridays. We can pick up some things at the farmer's market on Coast Village Road, and the rest we can find in the garden. Marge has a glorious, overgrown, hidden gem of a garden.

Come whenever. We'll be on kairos time.

Big hug,

x

PS—How wonderful your cousin is having a baby! Since the shower is soon and you're probably in need of a gift, I recommend you look for a snuggly stuffed animal with hangy-down legs to be easily carried and hugged. Ideally a bunny.

> Nothing is ever really lost, or can be lost,
> No birth, identity, form—no object of the world.
> Nor life, nor force, nor any visible thing;
> Appearance must not foil, nor shifted sphere confuse thy brain.
> Ample are time and space—ample the fields of Nature.
> The body, sluggish, aged, cold—the embers left from earlier fires,
> The light in the eye grown dim,
> shall duly flame again.

> *WALT WHITMAN*

CHAPTER 4

ON LOVE & CHOOSING

If you are not too long,
I will wait here for you all my life.

OSCAR WILDE

MARCH 29

Dear Ash,

I can't wait any longer. Tell me about this boy! He's a junior? What's his name? You've only spoken once, is that right?

I assume he's the same one you told me about in February, who sat next to you in English lit and asked to borrow your pen. Is that him? I knew some small flame was alight by the way you told the story. And now he's written you?

Great crushes make for great stories. For all the wonderful torture of feelings and butterflies and embarrassing fumbles, what other thing could make you feel like you're flying and falling and twirling all at once? Sometimes it's plain fun to have a crush. It gives us someone to dress up for.

When it comes to amusing romantic encounters, oh, the stories I could tell. Some were great crushes of my own, while others are tales of unrequited love I will never forget—more for their humor than any measure of actual romance.

Three Camels

After my first week in Jordan, so many things felt familiar. The hearty tang of hummus and the browned halloumi cheese, the mysterious eyes and curious glances of veiled women on the streets, the groups of young men walking through malls and cat-calling girls while holding each other's hands. I found this ironic because holding a girl's hand in public was completely taboo.

In Jordan, the locals drive as if they're still riding camels. In the desert days of old, my cousin Ruth explained, the camel with its nose farthest out always had the right of way. Whenever we came to an unmarked roundabout, I watched the cars edge forward in the dusty rush and, just like the camels in times gone by, the one with its bumper out farthest went first.

Camels became the theme of our trip, from driving alongside them as they ran down the highway's edge, to riding their wobbly humps through the burgundy walls of Petra. One morning we

My Bedouin suitor before the proposal. With his three-camel offering.

made the dusty, hot descent into that picturesque valley, where generation upon generation built cities into the carved mountain face heralded as one of the Seven New Wonders of the World. There we found a local guide to tour us around on camelback, and that charming Bedouin escort, just four-foot-something tall, decided an American wife was exactly what he wanted that day.

He offered my mom one camel for my hand in marriage: the happy animal she was perched upon. He could see she was quite taken with the animal.

"My daughter is worth more than *one* camel!" Mom exclaimed.

"Three camels," he countered, hands spread wide in an offering, "and my heart. It is all that I have."

Moved by the mix of unrequited love and pure emotion in his voice, Mom looked back at me in earnest. "Honey, they *are* really cute camels."

I laughed, in mild horror. She turned back to the expectant Bedouin. "That's a generous offer," she replied, "but there is no way my daughter is going to live in a cave." Which was, in fact, this Bedouin's address.

"Oh, it's no problem." He grinned. "I come to California!"

Thoughts on Love

So, my dear, since you seem to have love on the brain and I'm afraid you're going to start charging toward an MRS degree— because we've all heard the campus joke, "a ring by spring or your money back"—let's talk a little bit about love and marriage this month.

I'll begin with a few things I used to think.

I used to think relationships were only about finding the right person . . . until a mentor told me relationships are 50 percent about the right person and 50 percent about the right timing.

We can meet a partner who seems like the right fit at the wrong stage in our lives, at a time when we're not ready for a lifelong commitment. I've known fellows whom I could have dated, but when I was single, they were not. And vice versa. So friends we stayed. Right person? Who knows! But always wrong time. It wasn't meant to be.

I also used to think I had no control over that timing. But we do, Ash, to some degree. If you are caught up in dating the wrong person, in an on-again-off-again merry-go-round of heartache, how do you ever expect to meet the right one? You simply won't be available. Your heart won't be free to love the one who's right when it's tangled in the wrong relationship.

Many see breakups as a failure. Today I've come to see them as a success. Whether you get married to someone or not, the point is to see if you *should* get married. If you break up, you've found your answer. If you get married, you've found your answer. Success either way. Because if the answer is parting ways, you are now that much wiser and better prepared for what's next. Every relationship has the power to transform you and shape your character, even the unhappy and slightly more regrettable ones. As my friend Summerly reminds me often: every person who comes into our lives for a season has something to teach us.

Soul Mates

Ash, I used to think the goal of life was to find our soul mate.

Today, I don't believe that's true. It's not true because your soul is not incomplete until you find another half to make it whole. Are you half a person before you meet a partner, or decreased by half if the two of you part ways? Hardly. The truth is, no relationship will complete you, darling girl, but the right relationship will enhance you. It will magnify all the best parts and challenge all the bad. It will help you to blossom and bring you to life and make you *more* you. More of who you were designed to be.

You see, Ash, our souls are not a puzzle missing a piece. What if your soul mate was born halfway across the world, or died at birth, or married someone else, or lived in another age? We never find a soul mate, but we can find a mate for our souls. We can choose someone we connect with on the deepest level, who seems to understand our souls more than we understand them ourselves. We can choose a partner with whom our spirits will journey, so long as life allows.

Someone becomes a soul mate in the way two trees grow into one. Inosculation, it's called. Rooted individually but planted side by side, the two trees grow independently until one day— their branches touch. And then gently, as the wind blows and the time goes, their bark abrades and the inner parts graft and the two grow together, as one. On and on this entangling goes. From afar you still see separate trees: two trunks, two sets of roots. But up close you cannot tell where one tree ends and the other begins, so entwined they've become by the weather and the years and the necessity of leaning on each other. Sycamores do this, and willows and olives and ash trees, even.

Marriage trees, some cultures call them. Only an ax can break them apart.

And so it is with soul mates. We root ourselves beside another, and as the winds of life blow and the storms of life come, we grow together and intertwine until we forever grow as one.

Falling in Love

People talk a lot about *falling in love*, Ash. And falling in love is wonderful, exhilarating, addictive. A rush of emotional caffeine to the groggy, awakening heart.

I remember my first falling so well. Write to me about yours! I was sixteen going on seventeen, just like Liesl in *The Sound of Music*, and he was twenty-two. Dark and mysterious and covered in tattoos, Chris was the worship leader for our youth group. All the girls adored him, but for whatever reason, he gave his attention to me.

And I fell hard.

That crush, so sweet and innocent as our friendship grew, was, in fact, a tiny scandal in the youth group. High school students weren't supposed to *like* the leaders, and vice versa. So we waited. Which was hard—there's a reason the word *wait* sounds heavy. But wait we did, through long, arduous months of daydreaming and cryptic messages with Tony Bennett song quotes. My girlfriends and I would watch Chris sing, and he would stare out at me from the stage and my stomach would do triple-toe loops.

Those foggy summer evenings before my senior year, flanked with the freedom of newly minted driver's licenses, were filled with bonfires on the beach, deep conversations in the driveway, and swing-dancing classes downtown. I would wait through the rotation of fumbling dancers to meet Chris for a twirl before we'd rotate once again. As a leader, he couldn't take me on a date, so instead we all went everywhere together. For my seventeenth birthday he took our whole group of friends to a restaurant called Fleur de Lys, where we wore prom dresses and ate tiny dishes of unknown foods handed to us in unison from white-shirted waiters. I figured it must be the fanciest restaurant this side of the Mississippi. In the end, all of our friendships flourished that summer. I still wasn't convinced he liked me back, but the uncertainty itself was an adventure.

It was also the first time I opened my heart up to my mom.

She asked me about Chris one warm July evening as I sat on the living room sofa. I paused, debating whether I was ready to share the feelings churning inside me—and then I told her everything. We talked for hours that night, and many nights after. That summer my mom moved from being just my parent to being my confidante—my friend.

There was growth and beauty and goodness in the long anticipation.

That following Valentine's Day I went by Chris's office, still convinced we were only friends and I was reading into things, and it was the most natural thing to drop by on Valentine's Day. I brought him one white rose from my hostess job at Michael's on Main, and he played me a song he'd written called, "Waiting for June." The month when I would graduate. The month when he, the gentleman he was, would ask my parents for permission to take me on a date.

In that sweet, young-hearted moment I realized he probably—just maybe—actually liked me back.

Your List

What are your nonnegotiables, Ash? What do you want? What do you need? What will be your litmus test so that when you finally get to know this fella, you can know if he really is *right* for you? When we're dancing under the butterflies, it becomes very easy to know what we want and nearly impossible to know what we need. It's hard to see what traits we're overlooking when we so badly want some new romance to gallop forward on a white horse into the sunset.

I used to laugh at girls who made lists in high school with the qualities of their dream guy. Now, I think it's wise. I mean, if I make a list for the grocery store, why wouldn't I make a list for my future hubs? When I don't make a list for the supermarket, which I often don't, I usually go there hungry and come home with snacks and carbs and not much substance or produce or any of the ingredients I actually require for dinner that night. When it comes to marriage, Ash, we ought to know what we need, what we want, and what we absolutely won't settle for. If we know we want kids, why date a guy who is wholly uninterested in childrearing? If we know we're going gluten-free, why marry a pastry chef?

Let me be clear on one more thing: "Six foot two, chiseled abs, and croons like Sinatra" does not a good list make. If those are important qualities to you, put them in the "Nice to Have" column. But I encourage you to dig deeper. Describe his character. How does he treat his family? What about his heart? What are the qualities you won't budge on—or, when you see them in a man, will make your heart soar?

When my mom was in her early twenties, she got caught up in a toxic relationship. Her boyfriend appeared to be a charming, fun-loving guy throughout their first year together, but then something changed. He became someone she could no longer trust and soon began to fear.

After that experience, my mom knew exactly what she wanted. Three things, actually. She determined in her heart that the man she would marry would be honest, kind, and faithful. She met my dad around that time, when she applied for a job working at his family's business, a local art supply store in Santa Cruz called Palace. A starving art graduate, my mom figured she could use a discount on art supplies. Smart woman. The store manager went to my dad and whispered, "I think you should interview this one." She got the job, and later when my mom needed a friend to turn to, there was my dad. My honest, kind, and faithful dad.

You could say my mom married her list. And a lifetime discount on art supplies.

Working in Love

After so many months of liking, Chris and I did, eventually, date. We waited until the summer after my senior year, and it was awkward and wonderful and so much fun. We went boating on the lake and strolled the Santa Cruz Boardwalk and spent Saturday nights with our friends eating french fries in a red booth at Chili's. I loved everything about that senior year summer when crushing turned to falling.

What I know now, that I didn't know then, is that you don't keep falling forever. Soon the bright summer nights faded, as did the newness of everything, and we were left that fall with just ourselves and a relationship to tend to. I went off to college and he went off to art school and life got a lot more complicated for the both of us.

Ash, there's a reason why songs and movies and novels liken falling in love to a high. Falling in love releases serotonin to the brain—its own certain type of euphoria. The theme of so many daydreams and Jane Austen novels and rom-com box office hits, the very process of falling in love is addictive.

But there is another amorous stage, I've discovered, and it doesn't make many Top 40 hits. There is falling in love, Ash, and then there is *working in love.*

Working in love is where the relationship becomes *real*—a feeling so raw it burns. Working in love is when you have the choice to either run the other way, or run at something so much bigger than your individual selves. It's the point in a relationship when you decide the risk of leaning in is worth more than the security of standing on your own. You choose to trust. Working in love is when you fight, hard, but don't slam the door behind you. You stay, you learn, you get honest—with the other person and with yourself. You share what you feel at the core of your being, and the myriad life experiences that led you to that feeling, and you see what he does in response.

Does he listen? Does he hear you? Does he work in love too?

This, in some ways, is the most vulnerable love. When your emotional walls are about to spring up like battle ramparts, when every mechanism you've ever created to protect you from heartache wants to override the system, but you let that person in anyway. You know full well he could set fire to the motherboard, but you trust that he won't. And you believe that even if he does let you down, you'll be okay. Because you know how to heal, to forgive, to let go.

That, my dear, is working in love. And it ain't the stuff they show you in the movies.

In the Wall

As Chris and I passed that next year together as a couple, we had some incredible highs (skydiving!) but also some difficult lows—as most young loves do. He was burned out and I was overwhelmed and our relationship suffered for those and a dozen other reasons.

My church, Reality Carpinteria, was being built that year, and our community met each Sunday morning in a warehouse as the steel beams went up around us. I would go each Sunday with my roommates, and I'll never forget the first time Chris came with us. He didn't love it.

The church, just one year old, continued to grow my freshman year. The night before the plaster went up that spring, the whole church gathered to pray for the future of our community. I was handed a permanent marker, and as music played we wrote our prayers and the names of the people we were praying for beneath the beams.

I wrote Chris's name in the wall. We were struggling, but I loved him, deeply. I believed in him and I wanted God's very best for his life.

We broke up that following autumn, parked outside the Coffee Bean & Tea Leaf.

And you know what, Ash? I am so grateful we dated. I am grateful for the adventure we had and the lessons we learned and the friendships we formed in the process.

The truth is, in all of my relationships, wonderful as they were at the beginnings and as hard as they were in the endings, I've walked away thankful. My small cadre of suitors has shaped me, and challenged me, and pushed me. They've helped me discern who I am and to see absolutely who I am not. They've helped me discover who I want to be. I believe, with every fiber of my being, that we are better people today for having shared our lives for a season.

That's how I feel about Chris. We courted and we dated and we broke up, and I wouldn't change that journey for the world.

Aging in Love

Hugh, Marge's husband, passed away over a decade before I came to live on Hot Springs Road, and yet I feel as though I knew him. The warmth of his smile, his character, his affable approach. A pillar in the local community, Hugh embraced any quiet chance to help someone in need.

They were married late for their generation, Marge in her early forties and Hugh a few years older. They had courted on and off for years before that, their lives or locations or other romances always pulling them apart. Until one day, Hugh went all-in and declared his intentions, and the rest is history. Their love, which spanned four decades, was a romance for the ages.

My mom came down to visit me in Santa Barbara one weekend last year. It was the first time she and Marge had met. We sat together in the kitchen sipping coffee and chewing popovers hot from the oven as Marge shared long remembrances of Hugh. She rose from the dining room table at one point to clear the dishware and passed by his picture. Unaware of our watching eyes, Marge nonchalantly kissed her fingers and pressed them to Hugh's face behind the glass.

I want a love like that. Don't you?

To me, Marge and Hugh's love embodies a legacy. It was bigger than the both of them, and they poured out that love on their community.

That, sweet daydreamer, is the greatest kind of love. My favorite kind, and the one our culture so often forgets: *aging in love*. It's the twinkle in the eyes of a couple who's been married forty years, when they look at each other like they know something that you, young and naïve and supple-skinned as you are, cannot know and will not know until you've journeyed in love for as long as they have, many, many years from now.

If falling in love is champagne and a silk dress, then aging in love is a cup of chai tea and a cashmere sweater. Soothing, warm, familiar, with a spice all its own. A spice you've grown to enjoy as the sweetest of flavors.

Aging in love is seeing your partner one morning for the 48,924th time, and, with a breath of delight, catching a new fleck of color in their eye.

That's the kind of love I want.

Hold Loosely

Ash, this fellow—from what you've told me—truly sounds like a wonderful guy. And it was responsible of him to give you your pen back. But I must add briefly that just because he's a nice guy does not mean he's the *right* guy, or that this is the right season for the two of you. I hear you that you think he is perfect and probably your future husband. That's exciting. But you are also young and your world is changing and he is not the last great guy you will ever meet. I swear it.

Some say when you find the one who's right for you, you must hold on for dear life lest the whole thing slip away. But when it comes to relationships, I've found we can only hold one another loosely, with open hands and hearts. You cannot nurture a living thing by suffocating it.

Imagine your palms out, open to the sky, being filled to their brims with sparkling grains of sand. Have you heard this analogy? We'll imagine Jordanian sand, in honor of my Bedouin friend. This is your relationship, Ash, the object of your affection. Picture yourself squeezing the sand tight to protect it from spilling out. You grip it tighter and tighter. Most people don't realize they do this until it's too late, until the volume of the relationship has seeped through their fingers and slipped from their palms, cascading faster and faster toward the floor.

Hold your relationships—and in this case, your hope for a relationship!—with strength, poise, and balance. But above all else, hold it loosely, that you may hold it at all.

Be Your List

The great Ralph Waldo Emerson once said, "We must be our own before we can be another's."[1] Too many young women waste away their days dreaming about a partner who will make their dreams come true rather than building the life of their dreams. I've been guilty of this many times over.

I used to think the right man would bring my life excitement and community and meaning. I thought a man would be my adventure. Have you felt this way? Now, I've discovered I can make my own adventure. I'm building a life I love with all of those things. A husband shouldn't be expected to supply the life I want, but I pray—if that day comes—he will enhance it.

Once we've made our lists, the best thing to focus on is becoming the person a life partner of our dreams would be thrilled to marry. And trusting the imperfect process to get there.

Chris and I were never meant to get married, Ash, but we were meant to be in each other's lives. We had something to teach each other. I wrote his name in the walls of our church and walked away. Years later and two lives apart, Chris became a pastor inside those very walls.

Sometimes the end of the romance isn't the end of the story.

I've waxed poetic for long enough, so I will simply remind you of this:

You are worth it. You are worth fighting for, worth sacrificing for, worth the commitment, worth the wait. You, my darling girl, are worthy of adoration every single day, in every single way. You are worthy of a confetti-falling kind of love. And if you journey through a love that takes you separate ways, I believe you can endure the break. I believe your resilient heart will be all the more beautiful for it.

And, remember, in the words of Amy March, the youngest of the *Little Women*, "You don't need scores of suitors! You only need one. If he's the right one."

With that, I am off to make a list. I have nothing in the fridge for dinner.

All my heart,

x

To love at all is to be vulnerable. Love anything, and your heart will certainly be wrung and possibly be broken. If you want to make sure of keeping it intact, you must give your heart to no one, not even to an animal. Wrap it carefully round with hobbies and little luxuries; avoid all entanglements; lock it up safe in the casket or coffin of your selfishness. But in that casket—safe, dark, motionless, airless—it will change. It will not be broken; it will become unbreakable, impenetrable, irredeemable.

C. S. LEWIS

 CHAPTER 5

ON VOCATION & BEGINNING

How wonderful it is
that nobody need wait a single moment
before starting to improve the world.

ANNE FRANK

MAY 4

Dear Ash,

Greetings from London, sweet friend! I reread your last letter this evening. I needed that encouragement. You are so perceptive too—I've never seen my work that way.

London, by far, is one of my favorite cities in the world. Everything is familiar, but different. The very origins of our nation and culture are embedded in the life of this buzzing British metropolis. Big Ben keeps time over candy-colored phone booths as camel-coated Englishmen bustle to the tube and double-decker buses toddle along the wrong side of the street. I love taking pictures beside the Royal Guard. I can't imagine how anyone in a red cape and a foot-high helmet with a tassel on top could keep a serious face. It's a marvel.

I spent this afternoon with Sarah, the Duchess of York, working out new ways we can advocate for an end to modern slavery. The duchess is one of the most spunky, spontaneous human rights defenders I've ever encountered, having previously gone undercover to reveal a foreign government's horrifying mistreatment of disabled children in its state-run orphanages.[1] The children were dirty, malnourished, and tied to their beds. The duchess wrapped her head in scarves like a local and filmed the whole scene with a major broadcaster. That government now wants her indicted for the exposé. Seeing the risks the duchess takes and the boundaries she is unafraid to break gives me courage to be brave in the face of injustice.

Tonight I sat on a black iron bench in a green London square at dusk, feeling small in the face of great suffering and honored to work toward some common good alongside global movers like her.

After all, who am I?

The Start

Ash, in your last letter you said you wanted to know how I came to work in the anti-slavery movement, which takes me to these interesting places with even more interesting people. You want to know what plans and decisions I made in order to orient my life toward a meaningful career?

Well, the answer is simple, dear girl. I began with a twenty-year plan and worked backward.

I'm kidding.

I had no idea what I was doing when I started or how it would all weave together. I still don't, really. My mom says when you don't know what to do, you should just do the next right thing.[2] And when it came to my career, I suppose that's all I ever did. One next right thing after another, with endless mistakes and misadventures muddled in.

Frederick Buechner said, "Vocation is where our greatest passion meets the world's greatest need." I love that. But I'm also not entirely clear how we determine either part.

Many young people wait around to find their cause or their dream job, expecting some gold-plated door to swing open before them. But I've found that real-life opportunities are a lot less obvious and a lot more organic.

Sometimes in order to get somewhere, you start by just doing something. For me, that "something" was packing boxes.

It was the summer before my senior year, amid my fledgling employment as a part-time wedding planner, and I was attending a gathering with fellow comms majors that got me musing about my long-term career trajectory. I was chatting with one of the seniors and casually asked if she knew of anyone who needed an intern or volunteer who specialized in communications. After three years of study, I figured it was time to put my education to use.

Her eyes lit up. She had a friend who had an uncle who went to church with someone's cousin who knew someone who needed help marketing a new documentary called *Not For Sale*. Or something like that—I'm probably simplifying the connection.

I did know of the organization, I said. I had heard the founder speak the previous month at Westmont and had met him for a fleeting hello afterward. More than that, I'd had an interest in helping the cause of anti-trafficking for years.

One week later I was headed south on the 101 to meet the film's director at his Tuscan-style home in the warm hills of northern Los Angeles. We strategized and planned all day. I was to manage the marketing and partnerships for the documentary. I didn't know what marketing entailed, but I assumed I could figure it out.

Ash, I never planned to go straight into nonprofit work. Ever. When I was in high school and wanting to do something to stem the horrors of human trafficking, I imagined I could practice human rights law one day—after I'd made partner at a giant firm and amassed an exorbitant savings account. And yet, I cared deeply about the cause and knew how to do (or at least, assumed I could figure out how to do) something the cause needed. I could run the marketing for the small documentary that told the story of the book that had launched the brand-new organization of the same name.

I started doing something.

That autumn, I spent my afternoons packing small cardboard boxes at the local Read N' Post—because, it turned out, a lot of that marketing work meant shipping DVDs. It wasn't glamorous and it wasn't exciting, but it needed to be done. I called some techie Westmont grads to help me build a website and hosted screenings of the film. Two of the founders, Dave and Kique, came down to speak at a screening that October. I met them beforehand at Starbucks and talked their ears off about trafficking and porous borders in eastern Europe and what I thought we ought to do about it. I also, simultaneously, wondered who on earth I thought I was to talk like that to the experts.

We strolled together through Westmont's parking lot after the screening that night. "So, Allie—" Dave turned to me. "—what are your plans after graduation?"

The Secret

Ash, I am going to tell you a secret.

It's the secret of startups and companies, of masters and moguls, and of any wildly exciting career trajectory: *You make it up as you go.*

A typical backstage scene at an event with my boss, Dave.

Bobby Earle

That's it. You don't need to have it all figured out. You just need to start doing, and commit to constantly learning, and lead with humility in the face of everything you don't know.

My third week on the job I took a trip to DC, and given that I was now their first employee, the founders thought it'd be nice for me to check in with the state department's anti-trafficking office while I was there. We sat in black leather recliners around a shiny wood table in a windowless room, and an ambassador popped his head in at one point to say hello.

"How long have you been doing this?" he asked.

"Three weeks." I replied, to a few muffled laughs.

He grinned and leaned toward me. "Me too!"

Ash, as you grow in your career, you'll realize everyone else has—at one point or another—made it up as they go along too. Even if they are older or more educated or whatever. If you have confidence and ask good questions and act with integrity, it's astonishing what you can get done. Even when you're young, because youth is a valuable perspective.

Part of the learning process of careers is saying yes to every new challenge put before you. Now is the time! Why not try managing that project or tackling that goal or directing those volunteers? Carpe diem. If you fail, you'll know you failed nobly because you said yes. And if you're terrible at a thing, you'll know for next time. A lesson learned, regardless.

My first day at Not For Sale, the founders gave me the title of program director.

Program *director*. I was thrilled! I was twenty-one, and I was a director. High-kick. I hardly knew any directors, plus the word *program* sounded awfully critical to the organization's mission and success. Double high-kick.

My range of responsibilities was longer than my week's grocery list, but I said yes. I wrote the email blasts, managed the donation systems, and ran the online store. When we had events, I stuffed folders. When we got an office, I went to secondhand stores to find furniture. You name the job and I did it, because nothing was below me. Of course, this was helped by the fact that there were technically no staff below me, so delegating down wasn't an option. Instead, I learned how to do a little bit of everything, and it became abundantly clear where I excelled and where I did not. I suppose this was the benefit of starting young in a startup that lacked any traditional HR benefits.

Fast-forward six months, and I had the opportunity to lead a dozen students on a trip to Cambodia. A Westmont professor who happened to be a longtime friend of my boss at Not For Sale had joined us for part of the journey. They'd run a nonprofit together in Central America in their twenties. He reminisced and told me stories of the good ol' days, chuckling at one point that they named every new intern the program director.

"It was the catch-all job for everything the rest of us didn't want to do!" He laughed.

Cue the high-kicks.

The Key

When it comes to creating impact, the key is to do something. Start somewhere, Ash, and just show up. We think this means going halfway around the world, but often we can have the greatest impact just outside our door.

Which reminds me of my friend Caitlin. Who, in fact, has a thing for keys.

Caitlin was a singer/songwriter in Los Angeles and loved making jewelry on the side. A few years ago she started taking old keys and paying a locksmith to engrave them with inspiring words: *strength, hope, love, believe, dream.* She called them the Giving Keys because she wanted people to give them away when they met someone who needed the word. It turned out, despite all she invested in T-shirts and CDs for her merch table, the keys were always the first to sell out.

My friend Caitlin and I in the early days of the Giving Keys.

One day, while walking down the street in LA, Caitlin saw a young homeless couple sitting on the ground with a sign that read, UGLY, BROKE, AND HUNGRY. Being the sort of girl who never met a stranger, Caitlin stopped to say hello. She invited them out to dinner, hoping to give them some encouragement and hear their story. They were smart and funny and creative and kind. They also lived in a cardboard box inside a dumpster. Two hours in, Caitlin learned that the girlfriend, Cera, liked making jewelry.

That's the moment Caitlin's match of inspiration struck. "You're the missing link to the Giving Keys!" she exclaimed. "Do you want to be my business partners?!"

The next day Caitlin went to the locksmith to buy engraving equipment and Pep Boys to find hammers, and the couple started making the keys on the street. Eventually they saved up enough money to move out of the dumpster and into a motel, and then finally into an apartment. That was the most exciting key in those early days. Caitlin began hiring more engravers, each of them a person who'd had some hard knocks and wanted to transition out of homelessness.

The rest, so to speak, is history.

To Begin

Did you ever read those "Choose Your Own Adventure" novels in the school library, Ash? I would pore over them, drinking in the realization that we both choose our journey while our journey chooses us. At every turn, we make a choice, like Caitlin did, and from there the road unfolds.

But we have to move to make magic. We must open the book; we must turn the page.

Ash, as much as you dream and hope and plan to create, the world will always have a thousand and three things to distract you: a show to watch, a friend to call, a link to click. There will always be *something*. You will never have enough time or energy or motivation to seek every end you're inclined to pursue. You simply must decide to put some things first—to prioritize, dear girl. To determine what you're here for and take one step toward it. As William Wordsworth said exquisitely: "To begin, begin."[3]

There are many people with ideas but not many with impact,

because so few people have the courage to put their vision into action.

So dream, dear dreamer! But don't let the intoxication of your dreaming keep you from the moments of your doing. For what help to the world is a perfect product never sold, a good deed never done, an epic story never told?

I've heard soldiers are required to make their bed first thing every morning so that, whether they're a private or a four-star general, they begin their day by accomplishing something. I love that. Sometimes we just have to get something done.

Some days, Ash, you have to be your own motivational speaker. Some days you have to be your own personal trainer. You have to run beside yourself and chant orders like a drill sergeant or encouragements like a preschool teacher or growls like a zombie or whatever you need to do to make yourself keep going. Some days you've got to make your own magic.

Some days the most difficult part of the process is simply showing up. Some days the greatest accomplishment you can achieve is sitting down at your desk to do your work.

Or getting up to make your bed.

Gladiators

I don't know about you, but for me, Ash, one of the biggest hindrances to achieving my dreams is the way I seek approval from others. Especially online.

Have you seen the movie *Gladiator*? One of my favorites. If you have, you know the scene. The gladiator, dripping sweat and dirt and blood, has just given every last effort and conquered his opponent when, squinting, he looks wearily up to the stands where the emperor sits with his fist held out. Slowly, definitively, the emperor twists his wrist upward or down as the crowd erupts in applause or jeers in disapproving boos. Thumb pointing down to the pits, or up to the sky—signaling whether the gladiator lives or dies that day.

That, my dear, is how I feel after I make a social media post. Waiting down in the dust, looking up in vain, seeking the crowd's approval.

It's not a good look.

In the wild arena of the World Wide Web, followers, friends, and fans are as good as dollars. Having a lot of them gives you influence and options, but they won't give you joy. I wish I didn't care so much about what other people think of me. And worse, I wish I didn't look at them and envy their wonderful lives.

Swap Me In

I have wasted too many precious hours of this life wishing I could be somebody else. Nights lost in the social media feeds of women I will never look like, bodies I will never have, and places I will not be going—at least not this week. In those moments, my life feels pitiful and small. It feels like a trap, rather than something I've been entrusted with.

We cannot be anyone but who we are, Ash. We all know this, inside out and upside down. And yet, we still forget. *I* still forget. I try to be a better version of someone else rather than the very best version of me.

I'll see a superstar businesswoman or an actress or celebrity and think, *You know, I could do that just as well, or better, than she's doing it.* I literally have these conversations with God. "Hey coach!" I call to the heavens. "Swap me in. Let me take her position and lead this game."

The problem is, the universe already has her position covered.

The world does not need another version of that woman doing her life better with the same resources. You and I have each been gifted with talents and abilities and a perspective and a style all our own.

Spending your days trying to be someone else is like being an actor who only ever auditions to play the understudy. You may have a moment to shine, but likely not. If the understudy is your only aspiration, you will probably spend your whole career rehearsing for the mirror. And you, my darling, are a leading lady.

The Too Fairy

Ash, it seems to me a universal truth that as soon as we collect the nerve to seize our dreams, the Too Fairy comes along.

Yes, the Too Fairy.

The crotchety, cantankerous step-cousin of every fairy god-mother. The Too Fairy shows up uninvited to quiet moments of reflection, strolls behind you on walks to the corner store, and sits, rocking back and forth and musing, in the creaky chair by your bedside in lonely hours of the night when sleep evades you. For every dream or hope or challenge you have, she has her *too*.

You're too young, too old, too ugly, too pretty, too unsophisticated, too uncool. Too unskilled, too unschooled, too unwanted to ever be welcome. You name your aspiration; she'll crack her knuckles and snap back with her *too*. On it goes until the phone rings or the teller clears his throat or sleep finally sweeps in to save you. Then, leaving nothing but anxiety beneath your pillow, she steps back again into the shadows. To watch, and to wait, and to tap her wrinkly fingers to the cadence of your *toos*.

Sometimes, Ash, we have to name our demons. Sometimes, we have to put a face to our fears so we can look them in the eye and speak the truth into existence—telling the fear-crusted fairy we disagree and ending the conversation there.

Your Assignment

Comparison—wondering if you're not enough or if you're too much when held up to the standard of somebody else—is a paralyzing force in our world, especially for women and girls. Critics may clang from the rafters, but the voices in our heads can be the worst of all.

Comparison, it's been said, is the thief of joy. And joy is far too valuable for us to leave the door unlocked.

Rather than wishing our days away on someone else's more perfect existence, we need to own our personal missions, like soldiers in specific assignments. Lifelong missions from a general we can trust wholeheartedly, who knows each of us, our gifts, and our talents. There's something freeing in that.

That freedom—of living outside comparison—allows us to begin our custom-designed, uniquely assigned vocation.

And that is something worth making your bed for.

Onward—

X

> How we spend our days is, of course,
> how we spend our lives.
> ANNIE DILLARD

CHAPTER 6

ON INJUSTICE & MEANING

A propensity to hope and joy is real riches:
one to fear and sorrow, real poverty.

DAVID HUME

JULY 19

Dear Ash,

How is your summer, dear girl? How has the time been with your family?

I hope you're enjoying the simplicity of these days, rather than rushing through them. Enjoy the long afternoons and this quirky summer job and the fireflies under the moon. Because, before you know it, grown-up pressures will take their place, and you may miss the quiet hum of family days.

The Sickness

My senior year of college, I dropped my political science minor so I could finish classes a semester early. A tough choice, to be sure, but it allowed me to save money and take out fewer student loans and, most important, to start full-time work on this anti-slavery cause I cared so much about.

I began the position in January, and after walking with my graduating class in May, I hopped on an airplane to lead a group of students and fellow graduates to Cambodia. But not before sleeping through our graduation party—a side effect of the vaccinations I had. I figured it was worth it, though. I did not want to get sick.

Landing in Cambodia, we didn't waste a moment before diving into difficult things. We visited aftercare shelters and met with domestic abuse survivors and heard the grave stories of trafficking victims. We passed through crowded red-light districts, where rows of girls waited on cheap plastic chairs in rooms lit by sickly pink bulbs.

I met children whose families lived and scavenged in Phnom Penh's sprawling trash heaps. Families exposed to the rare and terrible diseases born in the remnants of rotting food and carcasses, of used hospital supplies and third-world discards. We could smell the place before we could see it, choking on the

Visiting Ta Prohm, one of my favorite places in Cambodia.

thickness of the air. Rounding the dirt path toward the entrance, I heard a *pop* and jumped—one of the girls had stepped on a dead rat, its carcass spraying remains across our feet. I gagged and moved forward. A dog was being roasted up ahead where small wooden stands framed the walkway. I wondered what they were selling—the items on display were all black. Walking closer, I realized it was produce, each piece covered solidly in flies.

I wore my leather Rainbow sandals that day in the trash heaps, and as we climbed the fifteen-foot mounds, their contents oozed around my bare toes. Poverty touched me that day, for the first time in some ways. I encountered it wholly, like I never had before, always viewing it safe from a distance.

Seeing these families and meeting their children, my first response was to get angry. *What sort of country lets its people live in its own waste?* I fumed. But days later into the trip, my perspective widened. I saw the dignity too. I realized these people were working. Away from the streets flooded with beggars, these were people trying to provide for their families in the best way they knew how: scavenging for recyclables and hunting for anything that could be salvaged. I was struck by the noble humanity of these communities in the midst of inequality beyond anything I was prepared to understand.

I was twenty-two and idealistic, and in those trash heaps I caught a different type of travel bug—one that no vaccine could protect me from.

I became sick at the injustice of our world.

Unbreakable

As much as the visit to the trash heaps impacted me, nothing touched me like the day we spent with the girls in the shelter of an organization called Hagar.

These girls were beautiful. Vietnamese and Cambodian. Raven hair, olive eyes. From eight years old to midteens. Spunky, graceful, delicate. Each one glowing from the inside-out. These were the most loving, most adoring girls I've ever met. Twenty-five of them, beaming, hugging, grabbing my hands and nestling their sweet faces under my arms. Exhausting every English word they knew to ask us questions, giggling and offering to teach me words in Khmer. Their joy was magnetic. These girls were full of life, energy, excitement, hope.

These girls were the survivors of brutal sex crimes. Some were rescued from trafficking, where adults sold their tiny bodies daily to the highest bidder. Some were auctioned by their families to locals who believed sex with a virgin could shield a man from HIV. Others lived in homes where their moms, destitute and desperate for income, allowed ravenous men to visit them and their sisters regularly.

These girls were the victims of rape. And not "rape," as the director explained to us carefully, but "RAPE." Violent, malicious, horrifying, all-capitalized rape. I felt nauseous as the thought settled into my mind. Several will never have children, their insides have been so brutally maimed.

Adults took the lives, the bodies, the spirits of these innocent girls and exploited them. Today, vendors along the streets sell cheap DVDs of horrendous child pornography—some displaying these very children—disseminated through communities like poison. Cambodians watch the videos in their open shanties, and the whole family sees. The children see. The neighbors see. And the fathers decide to try what they saw. Another child.

I can't express the rage, the heartbreak, I felt at the thought of what adults could do to these beautiful children. It wrenches me to comprehend the human capacity for evil.

And all the while—hope.

The Lotus

Ash, these girls now have light in their eyes. One of them once described her life to the others as being like a lotus flower. It grows out of dirty water, a dark and painful past. But it grows through it, out into the light. Its stalk is sturdy, strong—the flower blossoming grand with color and beauty.

The metaphor was so powerful they turned it into a dance.

The girls, glittering in silken costumes and elegant updos, performed it for us that afternoon. They began, poised with innocence as the lotus, and were slowly broken down by snakes and snails and sea-born creatures. Only to be rescued and brought together again by the saving fish, until they blossomed tall once more. At the end of the performance, the director asked if one of them would tell us what the dance meant. A small girl stood with confidence, her and her friends' eyes filling with tears as she relayed the metaphor in her native Khmer.

The director then turned to me and asked if I would respond on behalf of our group. I stood before these young girls, who'd just opened wide the pain and the resilience of their lives before

The girls at Hagar in Cambodia, performing the lotus dance for us.

us, and I struggled to express the lifelong impact their expression would have on each of us. As their teacher translated, I told them why we'd come. I told them why we wanted the rest of the world to know their stories. I told them why we needed their hope.

The Blessed Ones

I've never felt more immediately loved than when we headed to ice cream later that day. I was hugged again and again by these adoring girls, each looking half a decade younger than their age. I sat at a table with four of them, each wanting to know my favorite color, if I was married, if they could walk around the supermarket with me. They spoke little English—and I spoke even less Khmer—but it's astounding the depths that a smile can say.

The shelter at Hagar, which these girls now called home, reaches out to the poorest and most destitute women and girls in Cambodia. This children's shelter is only one facet of their remarkable programs and business initiatives. The girls are put through intensive schooling, two grades in a year, so they leave with a full education. For as dark as their pasts are, it's difficult to realize that these girls will end up leagues ahead of their Cambodian peers because of the care they now receive.

Today, they are the blessed ones.

Hagar offers holistic aftercare. As the girls go through healing and counseling, study and play, they are also enriched by the love of a stable community. In a culture that's taught them the pain of this life is caused by bad karma of the last, the girls are welcomed into the reality that an everlasting God adores them and desires to restore them from the sins of a horrifically fallen world.

Before leaving with a thousand "God bless you's," the girls I sat with told me their dreams for the future. One wanted to be a singer. The youngest, a hairdresser. The third, a doctor. The fourth, when it reached her turn, jumped from her seat and ran to the next table, whispering a question to the director. She came back with the largest grin. "NGO!" she declared.

"That is just what I do!" I exclaimed, heart bursting. "You will make this world a better place."

And I know, without a doubt, that she will.

Joy in Life

Ash, have you seen the movie *Life Is Beautiful*? Promise me you'll watch it if you haven't yet.

The story is about an Italian father and his son, who are imprisoned together in a World War II concentration camp. Amid constant terror, the father turns the harsh Nazi rules into a game, and the camp into a playground for his son. With jubilant, whimsical love, he devotes all his energy to creating an atmosphere of joy for his little boy to protect him from the horrors of the camp.

There is much for us to learn from the ways children see the world, in how they experience the exciting and hard and mundane. To become a joyful adult, one must grow in experience and wisdom while not losing one's childlike wonder.

There is magic in the world, Ash, even in darkness; and childlike wonder is available to all. Truly joyful people distinguish themselves from those who are convinced all of life is monotonous and meaningless. It's their ability to marvel at a spider's web after the rain, or a ray of light on water, or a bluebird's song in the morning.

All children are born with this sensibility. Many lose it

through the years, as it is chipped away by hardship and pain and unhappiness and loss. But those who hold tight to wonder inhabit a different kind of world. They live in a sand castle kind of kingdom.

I recently heard the story of a little girl who kept wandering into her baby sister's room each night. Finally her mother listened in. "Tell me more about God," the girl whispered to the baby. "I think I'm forgetting." Little children understand more of God in a way because they embrace the inexhaustible mystery of the unknown. The greatness of a palm full of sand; the closeness of the stars.

Primary Desires

I love that you're taking a course in philosophy, dear girl, and that it's causing you to think about the world in new ways.

One of my favorite philosophers is Viktor Frankl. Have you heard of him?

Like the little Italian boy and his father in *Life Is Beautiful*, Frankl was a victim of the Holocaust, which he describes in his poignant book, *Man's Search for Meaning*.

Frankl's thinking upended the popular psychology of his day. You see, Sigmund Freud had made his mark on the world by advocating that the primary desire of man was to pursue pleasure. Frankl disagreed. Instead, he argued the primary desire of every person is to experience a deep sense of meaning. Only when we can't find meaning do we numb ourselves with pleasure.

To find that meaning, Frankl said, we need three things in life: The first is a project that demands our attention, a reason to get up every morning. For you, that's your college classes in this season of learning, and the wonderful clubs and student groups to which you're devoted. The second thing we need is a community of people who love us unconditionally. Like your lovely friends, your family, and me. The third thing, I think perhaps the most profound, is a redemptive view on suffering—to be able to envision a greater purpose, a redeeming end, amid the darkest circumstances.[1]

You, dear Ash, approach the hardships around you with purpose, and I pray you will continue to do so during hardships yet to come. You are living a life of meaning and will do so ever more as you lean into these three.

New Day

Speaking of dark places, Ash, I want to say again that I'm sorry about how disappointing your project was. I know how much effort you put into it and how frustrating this must be. I'm so sorry, sweetie.

All I can say is, regardless of how bad it feels today, regardless of how dark and discouraging and constricting, by tomorrow today will have passed, and you'll be one day forward. Despite everything you do or don't do, you are locked within a world that will turn another day, will set another sun, will raise another moon. Your cells will grow and die, as will the flowers that surround you.

That is the glory of our world. You might bear the weight of life's woes on your shoulders, but you can bear it—because in twenty-four hours you will be, I guarantee, one day further along. The dance of life is learning how to watch the world turning amid your troubles. It's learning to catch that momentum and let it swing you forward. It's up to you whether you leap into that next day or crash into it.

Every single day is a new beginning, and in each you're guaranteed to be one day older and a few hours wiser. Every moment a flower will be crushed to the dust, and another will break through the dirt. A baby will burst into the world in tears, and an old woman will close her eyes for the last time in peace, as someone she loves holds her hand.

That is to say, tomorrow will come. And you, the beautiful human that you are, will be more resilient for having journeyed through the lessons of this hard moment.

Grace and peace,

 X

Lord, make me an instrument of Your peace.
Where there is hatred let me sow love;
Where there is injury, pardon . . .
Where there is doubt, faith;
Where there is despair, hope;
Where there is darkness, light;
Where there is sadness, joy.
O Divine Master,
grant that I may not so much seek
to be consoled as to console;
to be understood as to understand;
to be loved as to love.

ST. FRANCIS OF ASSISI

PART II

SOPHOMORE

CHAPTER 7

ON FEAR & WALKING

I can be changed by what happens to me,
but I refuse to be reduced by it.

MAYA ANGELOU

SEPTEMBER 17

Ash,

It breaks my heart to hear about your sweet friend. Thank you for telling me.

I can't imagine experiencing the things she's gone through and can only say how much it speaks of your relationship that she would share something so personal and painful with you.

I'm grateful she's been meeting with the school counselor. Please encourage her to keep doing so. Coming forward after all these years, to tell her story and begin the journey of healing, is one of the bravest things anyone could do.

I also understand, Ash, why you feel burdened as you process all of this. I want you to know that's okay too. You love and care for her so much—I've heard you speak of her many times. Your empathy, the way you share in others' joys and sufferings, is what makes you such a treasured friend.

I had wondered if I should share this story or not. I think it's worth telling you now.

The Parking Lot

I was in eighth grade when my mom first told me she had been raped. We were running errands together one afternoon and had just parked our clunky silver minivan outside Mervyn's department store. It was one of those nothing days, when the sun hangs low above the trees and the world is too quiet and the sky is an off-color shade of boredom blue. I memorized the pavement as she spoke: the cracks, the faded hues, the oil stain.

I had been babysitting a lot at the time, and I'd let the next-door neighbor, a teenage boy I hardly knew but who was a close friend of their family, come by the house one afternoon. He hardly spoke to me, and I thought nothing of it because he was always at their home. Who was I to say no? His visit concerned my mom, though, so she decided to break open some of the world's darkness and pour it at my feet that afternoon.

You see, my mom had been my age when she was sexually assaulted. Two of the popular girls in her eighth-grade class had decided to adopt her as a friend, and life seemed to be looking up for my sweet momma. She was energetic and optimistic and naïve. One day the girls invited her to hang out with them after school. When she arrived at the house, they told her to go into the shed in the backyard and wait for them.

A boy she didn't know was waiting there too. Waiting for her.

The girls had set her up.

My mom ran home after the attack and wept. She never spoke to the girls again, and she tried to bury that day and the hovering shame in the vaults of her memory. Life moved on. It was an entire year before my mom saw the word *rape* for the first time in the newspaper, before she learned there was a word besides *sex* for what had happened to her.

I was numb as I listened. Everything within me wanted to run from the passenger seat of our car, but I couldn't have moved if I tried. My mind spun and contorted, bending to make space for what she was saying. I knew that rapes happened to people, but I didn't know it could happen to my people. To people I knew, to people I loved.

My mom paused to let me process, to let me respond. Finally I choked out a question, the only one that floated past my reeling mind.

"What would you have done if you had gotten pregnant?" I asked quietly. My eyes were still glued to the windshield, staring down the pale cement parking space as if it were a raft that could carry us to safer shores.

She paused again, collecting words for the bleak answer she gave. "I would have killed myself," my mom said, resolute. In an era when girls who got pregnant were ostracized and sent away, all the fear and shame and social stigma felt like more than she could bear. To her, a child raped at fourteen, taking her life seemed like a better option than telling her parents.

I felt hollow. I still feel hollow, writing you now.

Twice More

But her trauma didn't end there, Ash. My mom was raped two more times after that, when she was in college. The details of those incidents, tragically and blessedly, she cannot remember— just the surrounding circumstances.

Her roommate's boyfriend and his friend came over one evening and made the girls White Russian cocktails. The next morning my mom and her roommate awoke disoriented and extremely hungover. They concluded they must have drunk too much, although neither remembered having more than one drink. They didn't even remember passing out.

The next weekend, the guys came over again. The night went exactly the same as before: talking, music, White Russians. But the next morning was different, because this time the guys overslept. My mom and her roommate, Mary, each awoke to find someone asleep next to them in their beds—Mary's boyfriend was in my mom's bed, and his friend was in Mary's.

Only then did the girls realize what had happened to them. They had been drugged and date-raped. Twice. But if *date-rape* was a term back then, my mom had never heard of it. The guys took off running, and my mom and Mary never saw them again.

It was years into my parents' marriage before my mom ever spoke with my dad about the sexual assaults. It was the first time she'd spoken of them to anyone. I was the second person to hear.

How many girls and boys, how many women and men, have suffered like my mom in their silence? "There is no greater agony than bearing an untold story inside of you," said Maya Angelou.[1]

I read recently, Ash, that one in five college women in the US are sexually assaulted.[2] One in five. How many of them speak, like your brave friend?

I remember the first time I drank a White Russian. It was at a bar somewhere in Belgium when I studied abroad, and guilt consumed me as I took a sip. I couldn't finish it. I felt sick with my mom's pain, sitting in the memories as if they were my own.

The Fear

Since that day in the parking lot in eighth grade, I've believed I would be raped someday too. It's not logical, and I don't think

I've ever told anyone, let alone my mom. I just carried it with me, Ash, like an eerie acceptance—the fear that what happened to my precious momma would one day happen to me. Because if anyone deserved it, I did. Not my mom. Not my gentle, unconditionally kind and loving mom.

I even feel guilty saying it out loud. I was not raped—my mom was. Some of my closest friends have been sexually assaulted as well. I have not. But it does not negate the empathy I experience, the pain of abuse I feel as I share in the suffering of the closest person in my life. I am spirit of my mother's spirit, blood of her blood.

Fear is an unwelcome friend, Ash. He sneaks up behind us quietly and stands too close, breathing his stale, cold breath down our spines. We can't alter him, but we can step away. We can look him square in the eye. We can confuse him or throw pillows at him or dance around him in circles and laugh at the absurdity of his lies.

But whatever we do, we must move. We cannot be paralyzed before fear, or else he'll just keep breathing. Too close. And all we'll know our whole lives is fear's stale breath.

We all have fear, Ash. Rational and irrational alike. What we do with that fear is what forms who we are.

The Reason

You asked me why I care about human trafficking and sexual exploitation, and I told you part of the reason why. But the real reason why is my mom. It was my shared suffering in her pain and shared journey in her healing that led me to this issue. All I could do to redeem what had happened to my mom and overcome my own fear was to serve others who were sexually exploited in some way. So I turned my energy toward it. I worked on behalf of those who were vulnerable to or had survived some abuse that I could hardly bear to imagine, and yet could not bear to ignore.

When my mom was pregnant with me, she attended her ten-year reunion at her former high school in upstate New York. There she saw the man who had once been the boy who'd raped her in the shed of that friend's backyard so many years ago. Now he was grown, perhaps with a job and a family, attending their high school reunion.

He approached my mom during a quiet moment.

"I'm so sorry for what I did to you," he said.

My mom nodded. It was all she could do. But it was a nod of forgiveness, acknowledging her pain and his tortured conscience, and maybe, just maybe, relieving them both of some shame.

The First Walk

Healing comes in many forms, Ash. Sometimes it's instant, sometimes it takes years, and sometimes it spans over decades.

My best friend Christie has been through a lot in her short life. Exploitative relationships, drugs, an eating disorder, abortion— all during her teen years and early twenties. Today she shares her story in schools across the country. I won't tell you more, because I want you to hear it from her face-to-face. You'll get along so well.

Looking back, I think walking has been the theme of our friendship—walking together through hard things, or in circles around Butterfly Beach when we just needed to process.

Christie and I met early on in my Westmont days, but we didn't become true friends until a few months before my graduation. It was Easter Sunday, and I was sitting outside in a sunny

Butterfly Beach. Where we loved to walk.

amphitheater at Reality's annual Easter service. My pastor, Britt, had invited anyone wanting to commit their lives to Jesus to walk to the front.

As the music lifted higher, swarms of people came down the aisles. The scene was beautiful. Just then I caught a glimpse of a golden-haired girl in a lavender dress walking forward. It was Christie. I watched her make the journey to the front, disappearing into the crowd of bent heads and lifted hands. I wasn't sure why I'd noticed her, since there were many people I recognized. But the scene of her walking forward stayed with me. It was like a tractor beam illuminated her in my mind's eye that morning, saying, "Pay attention."

Little did I know, that walk marked the greatest turning point of Christie's life.

A week or two later, we found ourselves at a barbecue and struck up a conversation— something we'd never actually done before. We decided lunch that week would be the best

Christie and I at Marge's house on Easter Sunday, one year later.

Katee Grace Clay

idea in the world, and then we never stopped doing lunches, or life, together. We were instantly friends, the way you instantly become a sister when your sibling is born.

The Life House

Christie and I always took walks together in Santa Barbara. Oftentimes because it sounded better than the run we had planned, and also because there's a reason why walking rhymes with talking. (I loved our walk in San Francisco, Ash!)

One of our favorite strolls was along Rametto Lane, the street in Montecito where Christie lived in a converted garage off the house where she'd grown up. Her mother now rented the house to a man named Chuck, who looked out for Christie and referred to me as the "porcelain doll" when I came by. Probably because I was pale.

The old ranch-style place sits back from the road and is guarded by a bramble of cream roses and a white picket fence. Christie never liked that fence. She thought a white picket fence represented a cruel fairy tale back then—two-by-four lies guarding make-believe stories of perfect childhoods that she, and others like her, had not lived. A pretty fence protecting brokenness.

There was, however, another house down Rametto Lane that Christie did love. Dearly. It did not have a fence and was under construction when we first became friends. It was perched atop a small plot of land with a view of the shimmering ocean. You could tell it was beautiful once, and could be beautiful again, but work was always being done, inside and out. It was still incomplete.

"That house is like my life right now," Christie would say as we walked by. I had never given the house so much as a glance till she mentioned it. It wasn't much to look at yet.

"I watch it every day," she told me, "and I'm reminded that

God is doing a work in me. Most of the old parts have been torn down and the broken things ripped out, but there's still a lot of rebuilding to do."

For Christie, God's work began when she made the decision to leave a series of unhealthy choices and relationships and walk down that aisle on Easter. You could've said I was a good influence on Christie through those years, and maybe that's why we came into each other's lives. But in fact, as these things tend to happen, she was the good influence on me.

A Magnitude of Grace

You see, Ash, Christie taught me about grace. While I was busy patting myself on the back for making seemingly good life decisions, Christie had her arms thrown open to the heavens, exposing her grief and her missteps and experiencing the unbridled fullness of God's love.

I marveled at her faith. It looked nothing like the religion I so frequently saw, and I wanted the vibrancy and passion that made hers so alive. Hers was the opening scene of a love story. It reminded me of the relationship I had with God as a child, an adventure that was wild and uncharted and free. Sometimes I felt like the older brother in Jesus' tale of the prodigal son, the one confounded by the celebration when his wayward sibling came home.

I'll never forget one of our small group gatherings that summer. We were crammed onto a deck with two dozen people talking faith and spirituality as the sun went down over the California Riviera. "I think God allows us to have a messy process so we don't forget our daily dependency on him," Christie piped up from the back. "If we thought we had it together all the time, we'd forget how much we need him day by day."

Guilty, I thought. *Party of one.*

I'd been living my life closed off to the magnitude of God's grace because I thought, quite simply, that I had it all together. I thought I was a finished product. You know, one that my family and God and the broader society could be proud of. The problem was, without thought, I'd pulled myself out of the fires of active faith, thinking I was cooked. I may have been comfortable, sure, but my soul felt flat and half-baked. Like a pudding that was supposed to be soufflé. Still chocolate, but something you'd send back if the waiter brought it for dessert.

Christie, on the other hand, was actively engaged in her journey. She was experiencing spiritual growth from the endless bounds of her admittedly imperfect, in-process life. Meanwhile I kept my head down, trying to look like I had it all together. When really—let's be honest—I never, ever did.

I spent the first year of our friendship learning what it meant to lean into my own mistakes, shortcomings, and needs. The sensation feels like diving into a wave. A scary, sharp blast of cold, then the most liberating rush once you come back up. I learned in those days, like I never had before, what it felt like to dive into grace.

When I picked Christie up from her home one evening, a year or so after that Easter service, she exclaimed, "They moved the dumpster!"

I looked at her, confused.

"The one outside my life house," she said. "It's still under construction, but the dumpster is gone now."

Keep Walking

I'm grateful you're talking to me about your friend, Ash, and I just want you to know it's okay to keep processing. It's okay for you to see a counselor too. Counseling can be so healing, especially when it comes to carrying something as difficult as your friend's story. I am a firm believer that shared sorrow is half sorrow, and shared joy is twice joy. But that still means, through empathy, you'll bear some of another's pain. That's both the burden and the gift.

I'm going to call you tomorrow to talk more. Know that I am here, if you need to speak before then. I know you've already offered her this, but she can always call me too. If it helps.

I'm proud of the kind of friend you are. Remember, don't try to fix anything; you don't need to right now. Just listen, be present, and walk with her. Sometimes simply showing up is the most meaningful gift we can give.

Love you, dear girl. Thanks for trusting me with the heaviness of life.

I trust you too.

x

PS—I came back through Santa Barbara last week. Someone has moved into Christie's life house, and lights were on in the windows.

> Today I know that such memories are the key not to the past, but to the future. I know that the experiences of our lives, when we let God use them, become the mysterious and perfect preparation for the work he will give us to do.
>
> *CORRIE TEN BOOM*

CHAPTER 8

ON IMPACT & BEARING

For to be free is not merely to cast off one's chains, but
to live in a way that enhances the freedom of others.
NELSON MANDELA

NOVEMBER 18

Dear Ash,

I'm so glad to hear your friend is doing well. What a blessing
it sounds like you've been to her. And she to you, as well.

You asked what I thought of Sweden, and I will say first of
all that it's breathtaking. Blue canals and cobblestone roads and
rows of trees and quaint Nordic shops. Everything is clean and
thoughtful and well designed, the streets full of young handsome
dads pushing strollers and enjoying their mandatory paternity
leave. There is even an ice bar, made out of ice, where you wear
parkas and sip drinks out of tumbler-shaped ice cubes. Sweden is
an enchanting place, but I hadn't come to see the beauty.

I was invited here by the Swedish government, believe it
or not, to observe the innovative models they've employed to
fight human trafficking. The Swedish Model, it's called. They
brought over a small group of journalists, and although I am

most certainly *not* a journalist and made that clear, communications director of an anti-slavery organization made the cut, so I came.

You see, Sweden, like most countries, has also been home to a dark undercurrent of exploitation. And the planners of our trip did not waste a moment in showing us their nation's work to combat it.

Upon arriving in Stockholm, we met with elected leaders, police officials, and social workers. We toured government buildings and nonprofit halls and trafficking shelters. We met with survivors. Many, I learned, had been told at thirteen that they were going to be dancers. They were "trained" for three months, their passports were stolen, and then they were moved through the EU, country by country, so the police could never catch their abductors. They were from places like Nigeria, Moldova, and Estonia. Some were now mothers. Some were still stalked by their traffickers, bearing marks on their bodies from the physical bondage they endured.

What Do You Do?

In the early days of my anti-trafficking work, I internalized everything. The stories I heard, the work we did. The heaviness of it all.

It didn't help that most people I met in those days didn't believe I was working on a real issue. So much has changed in a few short years, but back then, I doubt my own friends even understood what modern slavery was, let alone how prevalent it is.

I can be awkward during small talk at social gatherings regardless, and this made events and dinner parties all the worse. I dreaded that typical, looming question.

"So, Allie"—*Uh-oh, here it comes*—"what do you do?"

Suddenly, it felt like all eyes were on me.

"I work in anti-trafficking," I'd quickly reply. *There, I've kept it simple.*

At that point I would open my mouth to change the subject and be caught by the inevitable reply: "Oh, you mean, like, drug trafficking?"

Here we go.

"No, I mean human trafficking," I'd say, matter-of-fact. "I work against modern-day slavery."

At this point the inquisitor would either gently explain to me that we'd done away with slavery in the mid-1800s—*thanks for that*—or there would be a long awkward pause. A glass would clink, and then someone else would ask if I could pass the spicy tuna roll. It was rough.

I wondered, at moments, if I was going out of my mind.

Was I making all this up?

All of Them

But I wasn't making it up, Ash.

As I continued working, I'd hear more stories: the women who came out of brothels on the streets of Bangkok, and the fathers trapped with their families in generations of debt bondage in the brick kilns of rural India. I'd learn about the children forced to pick cocoa for our chocolate in Ghana, or cotton for our clothing in Uzbekistan, or mine minerals for our cell phones in the Congo. I'd hear stories from the countless teenage girls on the streets of Los Angeles who'd run away from bad homes and been picked up by pimps, sold night after night because no one ever came looking for them.

The greatest human ailment is apathy, and I knew too much to turn away.

When I went on that first trip to Cambodia, everything sank in deep. The darkness of the issue collided with the safe and stable life I'd left behind.

I'd expected to visit local anti-slavery organizations on the ground in Siem Reap and Phnom Penh, but our guides also spent time showing us the sociopolitical roots of the problem—namely, the countrywide genocide that had happened just three decades before.

The details of the Cambodian genocide under Pol Pot were gruesome, Ash; the reverberating effects on the country were chilling. I'd grown up learning about the Holocaust, but I hadn't fully understood that genocides still happen today. I didn't know that even after genocides end, their aftereffects continue for decades. In Cambodia, neighbor had turned against neighbor and the educated class had been slaughtered, creating a vacuum for staggering injustice and the commercial sexual exploitation of children long after the war was over.

One afternoon, the air heavy and sweltering, we visited the largest of the killing fields, Choeung Ek, where some seventeen thousand innocent people were slaughtered in the late '70s during the four-year genocide. The UN estimates more than two million people in total, over a quarter of Cambodia's population, were murdered in those years under Pol Pot's regime, the Khmer Rouge. They were the victims of religious, political, socioeconomic, and ethnic cleansing.

I stared silently at the mounds of dirt before us, where hundreds of people a day had been clubbed or butchered like animals and dumped in the ground. A seventeen-story Buddhist shrine stood in the midst of the mass graves—a monument of sorts—filled with thousands of human skulls excavated from the site. Their hollow sockets gazed out as we took in the scene.

"Why is there fabric down there?" I wondered aloud, pointing to the colored scraps of cloth protruding from the sunken earth.

"That's clothing from people buried here," explained our guide, solemn but matter-of-fact. "More of it keeps coming up each year."

Our small group also visited a former high school outside Phnom Penh, Svay Prey, with yellow walls and checkered tiles that had been turned into a torture and execution center by the Khmer Rouge. I could still see bloodstains on the floor. Of the fourteen thousand people known to have entered, only seven survived. We walked into a room plastered with photos: thousands of black-and-white images of prisoners who'd been held at the school. The snapshots were taken before each execution as proof to the Khmer Rouge officials. Local mothers and fathers and children with haunted eyes in ghostlike portraits stared back at me from their final moments. I stood alone in that room with our guide and slowly calculated his age.

"Did you know any of these people?" I whispered as we stepped into the stairwell. "Was any of your family . . . hurt?"

I almost didn't ask the question. How do you ask someone if his family has been murdered? But I've learned, Ash, when faced with hard circumstances, the worst thing we can say is nothing.

"Yes," he replied quietly. "All of them were killed."

I was silent as he told me of his escape as a small boy, hiding in neighboring villages and eating rodents in the fields to survive. He came to America as a refugee.

After I returned home from that trip, I visited my parents in Santa Cruz. We sat around the dinner table and caught up on the mundane until finally they moved to the obvious question at hand.

"So," my mom probed gently, "how was Cambodia?"

I thought about our guide, and the killing fields, and the families in the trash heaps. I thought about the hands of the tiny girls with unbreakable spirits who'd suffered such monstrous abuse. And for the first time in my life, Ash, I was speechless. Utterly speechless. I had seen too much, been exposed to such darkness, that I couldn't respond. I didn't have the framework yet to process what I'd seen.

I looked at my parents and shook my head slowly, stunned by my own loss for words.

There was nothing I could say.

My Breakdown

That fall, Not For Sale held an advocacy event in Washington DC. There we met with congressional members and their staffers and marched (well, walked in a line) with candles around the Capitol. Christie came with me for moral support, which made me feel like someone in my immediate world would finally understand the issue I was working on.

The last afternoon of the trip, when all the work was done and the exhaustion of the constant talking and sleepless nights had hit, we stopped by our musty budget B and B to rest.

Christie was processing the issue herself, having just spoken to some of the most powerful change makers in Washington on the subject. She mused over the scope of the issue and the need for legislation and pressed me thoughtfully with questions.

I told her how little we understood of a survivor's plight, of how we're all working tirelessly on this cause but have no idea of the realities the victims endure. The more I spoke, the more I worked myself up, until suddenly I was ranting. And then I was sobbing, curled in a ball on the bed.

Christie sat with me as the burden of the past year dislodged itself from my heart. She let me cry, and cry, and cry. At one point I caught enough breath to look down at the multicolored polyester bedspread.

"This thing is really gross," I said, blowing hard into a tissue as we both let out a laugh.

Christie and I didn't do anything to change the course of history that afternoon, but something inside me changed. I realized, for the first time, what an unbearable burden I was putting on myself in my attempt to save the world. It felt like going on a yearlong trip and trying to carry everything I'd packed in my arms, rather than wheeling it all behind me in a suitcase. Still a heavy load, but moved with ease, because the burden is where it belongs.

Gus Dizon

One of my first times speaking for NFS. I thought it was my job to save the world.

I realized, perhaps for the first time, I'd been trying to be a superhero instead of a servant.

Making Waves

Ash, I come from Santa Cruz, a place where surfing is more than a pastime. It's sacred. There are basic concepts every surfer knows, like how to pop up and keep the right of way and duck-dive or turn-turtle when the set is too big. But the most basic and obvious law of surfing is this: Surfers don't make their own waves. They participate in the movement of the ocean.

I have found the same law applies when it comes to making impact.

You see, Ash, in surfing, you don't splash around to build a swell. That would not only be fruitless, it would be ridiculous.

Yet many people wanting to make worldwide change do just that. They splash around in the water, trying to make waves.

A good surfer, on the other hand, gets to know the ocean. She waits for the tides, anticipates the swells, and watches for the waves to come in. Then, when the swell does come, she is ready. She spins around in the direction the set is moving and begins to paddle as fast and as hard as she can until the wave comes in behind her and lifts her up—shooting her forward and carrying her smoothly in the cradle of its force.

Sometimes the surfer rides gracefully toward the shore. Other times she tumbles. She loses her balance and lurches headfirst into the churning sea. She is flipped upside down and swallows salt water and feels like she might drown. But then she comes up for air, coughing and laughing, and jumps back on her board to paddle out again.

To wait for more waves.

I've realized, Ash, as I look back on those early years, that I was trying to make my own waves. I was trying to carry myself, to walk on water alone, rather than see the greater mission and purpose of which I was a part. I had to realize God was making the waves. I had to trust God was driving this social movement, and the invitation for me was to participate.

It is not on us to change the world, Ash. That is too great a burden for any one person to bear. But it *is* on us to improve the world. We can leave it a little bit better than when we found it. As Gandhi said, we can be the kind of change we wish to see.

When I began to trust that a good and loving God was moving in the world—with or without me—I felt freed up to join something bigger than myself. The weight of the issue remained the same, but the pressure fell away. The burden became lighter.

It's not on me to move God. It's only on me to look where he is moving and to move with him there.

Bear the Beams

There is a framed needlepoint piece in my bedroom that has hung there since I was a baby. It reads:

> We are put on earth a little space, that we may learn to bear the beams of love.[1]

Learning to bear the beams of love, in many ways, is the essence of life. It's what I have been doing all these years with my mom and with Christie and with the people I met in Cambodia and Sweden. We must learn to love, Ash. We must feel. We must be open to knowing the full weight of the pain that this broken world brings down onto others. Onto us. We must walk with people in their hurt, taking one step at a time and trusting that showing up for someone may be the very thing they need most to get through the day.

We must also learn to bear it well, and not in our own strength. Bearing it makes us human, because it heals our hearts and the hearts of others. We must bear the pain and not turn away, because those beams of love are why we're here.

When you come visit Santa Cruz, I would love to take you surfing.

Until then,

The needlepoint that's hung beside my bed since I was a baby.

Come to me, all you who are weary and
burdened, and I will give you rest.
JESUS OF NAZARETH

CHAPTER 9

ON FRIENDSHIP & MISSING

My friends are my "estate."

EMILY DICKINSON

JANUARY 18

Dear Ash,

I understand why you're starting to feel homesick. You're back at school after a long holiday break and feeling far from home. I've never been to your town, but I can understand why you miss it so much. Why you miss your community.

Have you heard of FOMO? I'm sure you have. *Fear of missing out.* It's that sinking in our stomachs when we learn that every one of our closest friends is attending a concert while we're sick at home in bed.

I think there's another kind of FOMO, though—one that you're probably experiencing acutely as you settle back in after the holidays with your family. *Fear of missing others.*

I'll never forget packing one evening as I prepared to leave for a business trip. I was making dinner and bustling around the house and relaying the details of my travels to come in the week ahead. My roommate Ruby paused midconversation.

"Allie?" She tipped her head to the side. "Aren't you going to miss us?"

I considered this for a moment. I was so excited for my upcoming plans and the friends I would see in Los Angeles that I hadn't really thought about it.

"Well," I reflected, "yes. Yes, of course I'll miss you girls."

Then I started processing. "But, wherever I go, I'm always missing someone. If I'm here with you, I'm not home with my parents in Santa Cruz. If I'm home with my parents, I'm not with my college friends back in Santa Barbara, or my brother working in Haiti, or my cousins in Atlanta.

"Being somewhere means always missing someone."

I'm not sure this satisfied Ruby, but it settled something in me. At some point I'd resigned myself to a certain type of nomadic life, which meant I would always be apart from someone I love. I suppose I could have prevented this years ago by going to the community college and renting an apartment next door to my folks and never going farther than the grocery store. But from a young age, I knew that, in order to be me, I had to leave. I knew there were aspects of who I would be—who I needed to become—that could only be achieved in places farther south on the 101, and ten thousand miles away across the ocean. If I wanted to be present in those places, it meant I would inevitably fall in love with the people I met along the way: host families, and travelers, and roommates, and adopted grandmothers.

Loving them all would mean being without them all, at one point or another.

This, dear Ash, is the joyous burden we bear in order to live a big life. If you love just a few people conservatively, you may have more ease, but your world will be so much smaller. Remember that when you're missing home this month.

Missing someone is a symptom of loving them, and we hold

the pain of missing in tension with the joy of loving whenever we are away.

Buddy

One of my first friends at Westmont was Ryan, whom I took to calling "Buddy"—because that's exactly what he was to me. He asked me for a haircut during the first month of freshman year, and although I'd never cut someone's hair before, I happily obliged. I was determined to not give him a mullet, so the whole endeavor took two hours. But, it turns out, two hours is ample time to make a friend, and he's been my buddy ever since.

Ryan was doing a master's program in England when I took my trip to Sweden. When he heard I was coming, he booked a cheap flight on Ryanair—pun unintended—to visit me on the last day of the trip.

"Are you sure you want to come *all* the way over here, just for a day?" I asked.

He was sure.

When I met him in the lobby and jumped into his hug, you would think he hadn't seen a human in months, let alone a friend. I pretended not to notice he was tearing up. Ryan had always been the life of the party, the center of attention. He was Cookie Monster in the freshman boys' Spring Sing performance when they chose a Sesame Street theme, for goodness sake. I had never seen him cry.

But in the words of John Donne, "No man is an island, entire of itself."[1] And Ryan had been quite alone during his time on the British Isle.

In those months of graduate school, Ryan had found himself lonely for the first time in his life. It was dark and cold, and his long-distance girlfriend had decided things were not working out and put an end to the relationship. Ryan was crushed and had fallen into a very dark place.

I've been in that place too. After my last breakup a year ago, I felt something I had never experienced in my short life: depression. My body was so heavy, my mind so dull, that it took everything in me to climb out of bed in the morning. Or at noon. Several of my closest friends moved away, and I had moved into a new house with girls I liked a lot but didn't know well, and I slid into a sticky, bitter lump of loneliness.

What surprised me most about that season was my inability to reach out. To call a friend, to say I was in need, to surround myself with people. I simply could not find the strength.

But Ryan did. His strength was a flight to Sweden to be with a friend who reminded him of who he was, where he came from, and what he loved. One day to fill his tank with joy—and that is what we did. I in my red peacoat and he in his trench, we wandered the winding streets of Stockholm, exploring Viking ships, shivering in the ice bar, and jumping in the leaves as they fell.

We are not designed to go this life alone.

Three Friendships

My pastor, Britt, once shared an interesting framework of relationships that has always stuck with me.

He said that in order to have a healthy spiritual life, we need relationships that look like the apostle Paul's: those who mentor us (Ananias to Paul), those who are peers (Barnabas to Paul), and those whom we mentor (Paul to Timothy). These dynamics balance our relational and spiritual selves like the three legs of a stool.

So many people surround themselves with only one or two

types of these relationships. They have tons of friends and peers, but no one wiser speaking into their lives. Others have mentors but fail to give the same care to those who are younger or less experienced than them.

I had the opposite issue in college. As an RA in the dorms, I was surrounded by young women who wanted my guidance and counsel. I was only months older than some of them, but they jokingly referred to me as "Mom." Ha!

I had teachers and adults around me, of course, but I lacked the older women in my life whom I could actually call on as mentors. Besides my momma, of course. I needed wiser women who were a little farther down the road, who could see things I couldn't see and draw on experiences I didn't have. Like sea captains who'd already been across a dozen oceans and had the cheap tattoos and siren sightings to show for it.

The threefold ideal isn't a rule for categorizing all friendships (God forbid we make a science out of it), but rather a model for orienting your expectations in relationships. It's also less about age than it is about the dynamic you have in your friendships.

I have a number of friends who are older than me, whom I love and adore, who, when we get coffee, mostly need to process and vent and get my advice and talk about themselves the whole time. This would be hard if I expected them to be mentoring or guiding me. I'd leave pretty deflated. But my expectation for these friendships in this season is that they really need me to pour into them, and that's okay.

It's not okay, however, if I don't also have people pouring into me. Make sense?

As you're seeking new friendships and relationships this year, I would challenge you to think about which of these areas is weakest, Ash. I could take a guess.

Just as I'm mentoring you through these college years, search out younger women for whom you can do the same. Not that you need to chase them down and corner the poor things in the dining hall, but do keep your eyes open. See if there's someone who resonates with you, who needs you in some way.

In Your Boat

Ash, do you remember that story in the Gospels when Jesus walks on water, and then Peter does the same? I always thought I knew that story inside and out, until one day my friend, Brant, gave me a new perspective on it.

He said that when most people read or teach this story, they focus on the strength of Peter's faith. Understandably so: it would take some guts to walk on water! Yet like a movie scene shot from only one angle, this perspective leaves out some other pieces of the story. In this case, the group of people standing behind Peter get lost in the scene—the other disciples. They are there watching Peter, supporting him, believing in him, cheering him on, giving him the courage to do the impossible.

They are the friends in his boat.

Not long after I heard this new interpretation, I was standing in my San Francisco kitchen on the phone with my friend Esther in Colorado. We'd met through a mutual friend at a conference and just, you know, clicked. She was a like-hearted person I wanted to live next door to and do life with. Thankfully, social media kept us sporadically up-to-date on each other's journeys, and then we caught up on the phone when we could.

Esther was going through an awfully hard season between work pressure and family strife, and I was under more stress than a mouse beneath a cat's paw. Our apartment actually had mice at that time too, which added even more stress. I mentioned the story to her briefly before we jumped off the phone. The Peter story, that is—not the mice.

"I love that," she mused. "And, I'm in your boat."

After that, it became a mantra for our friendship. Missed airplanes and bad reviews, professional failures and tense decisions: we were in each other's boat. Usually it was as simple as an email—"In your boat!"—or a text with the rowboat emoji. A small show of support in the friendship. Somehow it was much more nuanced and thoughtful than "You got this!" or "You'll be in my prayers"—the kind that you forget to pray anyway.

Soon it became the reverse: "I need you in my boat." Which usually got me praying, right then and there.

There are friends of circumstance, with whom we grow in relationship by the very nature of their proximity—roommates and family members and fellow students. Then there are friendships of intentionality. You never have the luxury of going to the same school with them or working at the same company as them or living near them, for that matter. In either case, I've found, the intentionality is ultimately what makes the friendship flourish.

And, when waters get rough, the ability to stand in each other's boat.

Gracias

When I was in high school, our youth group took a trip to Tijuana, Mexico, to build houses. Did you ever do any trips like that? At first I thought we were the most selfless, magnanimous group of students to be spending our spring break this way—until I got to Tijuana and realized how bad I was at building houses. I began to wonder if the trip wasn't more about building my character than it was about serving the world with my construction skills.

That was a humbling revelation.

I went back to Mexico a few years later on my junior year spring break, this time to Ensenada. Westmont takes a big group of students every year—and I saw it as a rite of passage.

We were given the opportunity to apply with any one of the volunteer teams and, being the overachiever I was, I chose the hardest one: the medical team. I imagined myself triaging patients and saving lives.

Now, *why* I thought I would make a great addition to this team, alongside the trained dentists and pre-med students, is still a mystery to me. As it turns out, it was a mystery to the trip organizers as well, and they stuck me on a more fitting outpost instead.

My shoulders slumped when I read my assignment: *haircutting*.

The haircutting team traveled alongside the dental team and gave free haircuts outside the medical clinics. I had only given two haircuts in my life: that one to Ryan, and the other to myself freshman year when I had no income. My split ends were frayed like a broom, so I'd stood in front of the mirror with my ponytail in hand and chopped an inch off with my desk scissors. I considered both cuts a success, and when I learned I'd be on the haircutting team, I began practicing and training between classes on any student who'd let me use them. I wasn't saving lives, but I was styling them.

When we got to Mexico, I was surprised how much joy something simple like a haircut could bring people—especially kids. I was helping where I could, but questioned how much of an impact I was really making in comparison to the doctors and dentists who'd left their practices to join our team in the clinics.

Until the last day.

The line for haircuts had dwindled, so I'd made my way past the triage area and into the clinic to see if I could be of service somewhere. Then I saw her.

A middle-aged woman with a troublesome molar sat in a

chair at the back of the clinic. The volunteering dentist didn't speak Spanish. He was harried, exhausted, and a little too gruff at the end of a long, hot day. I saw fear behind the tears welling up in her eyes.

I neared, watching for a moment. More students had gathered round to assist the dentist as he struggled with the difficult procedure. Finally, unsure how else to help, I did exactly what I would have wanted her to do for me in that moment. I reached out and grabbed her hand.

She clung to me tight.

I suppose my hand was something human in that moment. She held on until the tooth came out, and the entire dental team erupted into applause as the dentist beamed, relieved at his success.

Brow misted with sweat, I watched as a tepid smile of relief found its way to her face. Then her eyes wandered to mine amid the celebration. "Gracias," she whispered, so softly I had to read her lips.

I was no expert in that moment. I had no great skills and so little to offer—only my hand.

I don't know who that woman was, Ash. I don't know her story, or her family, or her dreams. I wish I did. But the clinic was closing and the cars were waiting, and I was rushed out just moments after the whole ordeal took place. All I can hope is that a hand, in that moment, was what she needed. Her simple whisper of gratitude will always be a reminder to me of why we care for one another. Though divided by geography and circumstance, we all want the same friendship, love, and human touch.

I think long-term friendships, like the kind my team leaders had within the Ensenada community, are the foundation for sustainable impact. Friendship is where we start. It's neither flashy nor applauded, but it's real. Sometimes we can't offer sophisticated solutions or massive financing or even great skill.

Sometimes all we can offer is our humanity. If we want to make social impact, we must begin with something social—we must begin with friendship.

Sisters

Speaking of friendships, I got your message yesterday about Emma. Without knowing more details, I will simply tell you this: I believe God gives us the family he does in order to teach us how to love others. Oftentimes, those family members that we must learn to love are people quite unlike us. Or, in the case of your sister, too much like us.

I would go so far as to say this: If you have difficulty loving a certain type of person well, a person like that is probably going to be in your family. Or in your extended family, when you get married someday. Rather than complain about someone who's in your circle for life, or even a season, see it as an opportunity for your heart to grow. Yes, maybe that person should be less manic or worrisome or argumentative, but maybe you need to learn how to be more caring or understanding or patient. Maybe you need to learn how to listen. Maybe they have something to teach you.

It's our life's privilege to love people, Ash. Our friends and our family and our community and strangers alike. It's an honor to participate in their stories. So, remember birthdays. Handwrite thank-you notes. Be intentional. Remember what your friends and family love, and surprise them with those things. We cannot pretend to care for the world if we do not care well for those we love.

And when it comes to Emma, remember, sweet Ash, she is only fifteen. She really looks up to you, whether you realize it or not.

Ever your friend,

X

PS—I can't wait to meet this new classmate of yours. Peyton, is it? She sounds caring and intentional and hilarious—the very best kind of friend.

PPS—Check your mailbox next week.

> We don't have a word for the opposite of loneliness, but if we did I could say that's what I want in life. . . . It's just this feeling that there are people, an abundance of people, who are in this together.
>
> *MARINA KEEGAN*

CHAPTER 10

ON WANDERLUST
& EXPLORING

We shall not cease from exploration
And the end of all our exploring
Will be to arrive where we started
And know the place for the first time.

T. S. ELIOT

MARCH 12

Dear Ash,

I love, absolutely love, that you're thinking about doing a study abroad semester. All of the programs sound incredible—I don't think you can go wrong.

Can you tell me a little more about the factors you're weighing in the decision? What's important to you, dear girl? What do you want most? I'm so proud of you for jumping into this adventure. The risks that make you giddy and uneasy and altogether overwhelmed become the adventures that shape you and the stories you'll share for a lifetime.

All Abroad

I was a sophomore—like you!—when I decided to study abroad. I wanted a lot of things: to live in Europe, to order fancy pastries in French, to study other cultures and political systems and international relations. I wanted to travel widely, to as many countries as would have me, but I didn't want to be confined to a bus of American students looking as local as a herd of sheep in a shopping mall. I wanted to live with a family, to learn about their world and way of life, and to challenge my norms—all while seeing everything we ultimately had in common.

This specific list of criteria led me to one option: Brussels.

The capital of Belgium and what many call the heart of Europe. Home to the European Union, Brussels is a hotbed of European history. I double-checked the location on the map: smack-dab in the middle of the continent, which meant short flights and train rides to new landscapes on weekends. Perfect! Plus, I liked the way the word *Brussels* rolled off the tongue. The fact that most of my peers didn't know where it was gave me a tiny twinge of satisfaction.

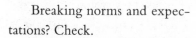
The Grand Place in Brussels.

Breaking norms and expectations? Check.

The program in Brussels was a once-in-a-lifetime chance to study international relations on the ground, to work in European politics, and to travel—and learn!—extensively. But an equal draw was the fact that the program was run by a university out of Washington DC, and I'd be the only Westmont student taking part. Little did I know, I was also the only West Coaster—and the only comms major at that.

Fish out of water? Check, check.

Who I Was

The other reason I wanted to go abroad was a headier one. Or heartier, you could say, in the nonculinary sense of the word. I finally felt like I'd hit my stride, which meant it was time to move. I was the RA for a brilliant and boisterous band of freshman girls in Clark M, had a solid group of friends and social functions on my calendar, and knew a respectable number of students on campus. Even *seniors*. I would wave to them as I strolled by, thinking in amazement that I was not the timid freshman of yesteryear. They would smile and wave back because they didn't realize how uncool and awkward I actually was. *I hope no one tells them*, I'd think.

But amid hitting my stride at school, I was hit with a reality that scared me more than all the early woes of adjusting to collegiate life: I was comfortable. *Really* comfortable. It meant I was having fun, but I wasn't growing. At least, not with the familiar aches and pains that prove real work is being done.

The more I thought about who and where I was, the more I began to wonder if I was simply a product of my environment. Was I making certain decisions simply because they would be affirmed by the world around me? This was a social crisis, to be sure, but it was also a crisis of faith. Was the religion I'd clung to like a childhood blanket only a reflection of the culture around me?

I wanted to know who I was. I mean, who I *really* was, outside the daily affirmations of the environment and community

I'd created for myself. I figured, what better way to find out than to drop myself in the middle of a new continent and simmer in the hot water of uncertainty for four months?

In the Woods

What was it like to study abroad? Oh, Ash, there are so many stories I could tell you.

My months in Belgium were a cocktail of glass skyscrapers and ancient ruins and sprawling European landscapes. But thinking back on that season now, the place that defined it most was the woods. The Belgian forest spanned behind my home in a little area called Ixelles, just off the tree-lined lanes of Avenue Louise. This was where I would often walk and pray and lose myself in time and place. It was here that my host sister, Clementine, and I would run the family's lazy old Lab, Butch, who I often confused with the American president whenever she and the family would call him by name. *"Boosh!"*

Some evenings we'd stroll so far we'd get lost, wandering past the old abbey into fields and horse arenas and dusty clearings, then scrambling as the sun slid behind the trees to find our way out before dark.

I suppose getting lost was the hallmark of my trip.

Lost in a directional sense, yes. I was always getting lost in new cities and street markets and bustling squares, whether I meant to or not. But I also got lost in a bigger way. Lost in the world as I'd known it. I found myself far from the confidence of knowing the local language, or the public transit system, or the cultural cues. And in that sense of lost-ness, the constant challenge of simply living in a different nation brought a new wonder back to my life. I existed in the charm of the unfamiliar, like a toddler discovering the world around her for the first time.

That's why I love travel. The very discomfort we work so diligently to shield ourselves from at home will ultimately become the experiences that transform our thinking, if we only lean into the discomfort.

The Pheasants

One autumn afternoon in Belgium, I met a friend of my host family who, taking pity on my lack of "proper" upbringing, invited me to come on a pheasant hunt. At a chateau near the French border, no less, because where else does one hunt for pheasants? I went, of course, but not before my host family dressed me in a suitable coat and Wellies. I was not allowed to go if I did not look the part.

We left before dawn, and the morning went well enough. The women stayed back with wicker baskets of croissants while I trudged through mud with the tweed-coated men. We moved up hills and through trees as "beaters" banged the thickets and pheasants sprang up toward the sky. Then wailing, obedient hounds would scamper forward to collect the falling birds from the brush. Everyone knew their part and I, for one, thought I had done a pretty good job at mine. Mind you, I wasn't allowed to shoot a gun or do anything particularly helpful, but I could provide moral support and I felt like I was fitting in. I was wearing a Barbour coat, for goodness sake! They probably thought I did this on weekends.

But Ash—then there was the luncheon.

We trudged into the chateau at noon, everyone discarding muddied boots at the door. Being the respectful guest I was, I did the same. That's when I noticed everyone else was slipping into *another* pair of shoes, formal shoes. Loafers and the like. I had been so proud to have found the right boots in the first place, I hadn't even thought of bringing dress shoes! I looked down at my socks: argyle, matching. I have a thing for argyle socks, because they always make your feet look a bit dressed up. So really, how bad could that be?

The friend who'd invited me looked momentarily horrified when he realized I had nothing to change into. "Just don't let my mother see!" he whispered, as if I'd forgotten my pants.

I shuffled sheepishly into the dining room, certain no one had noticed. My feet would be under the table, anyway. Then I saw the rows of shiny silverware and forgot for a moment about my shoes. Everyone ate with a fork held gingerly in the left hand, knife poised like an orchestral wand in the right. That seemed a bit awkward, as I'd grown up eating quesadillas with my hands. But I followed their lead and pretended it came naturally. Fake it till you make it, right?

With laudable focus, I landed a piece of lettuce in my mouth when suddenly I realized the conversation had turned to me.

"Maybe next time the American will bring her shoes." Roars of laughter erupted around the table, and my cheeks bloomed as red as the radishes. You can take the girl out of the beach town, but you can't take the beach town out of the girl.

The Same Me

I visited the Royal Palace that September before it closed to the public for winter. That palace is every fairy-tale dream I'd ever harbored in my childhood imagination. Wide, winding staircases, rich ruby carpets, and dozens and dozens of chandeliers. If you're quiet enough and listen with your ear tilted to the ceiling when the tourists clear the room, you can hear the whispered song of crystals singing as they softly rock back and forth. The clinking champagne flutes of fairies.

You see, my host father had told me to listen for the chandeliers—he'd spent many quiet days at the palace restoring antiques. He told me this in French, which I was slow at understanding, but the meaning clicked when he danced his fingers in the air and made a twinkling sound.

"*Ah, bon!*" I exclaimed—more giddy that I'd understood what he'd said. The Belgian accent is tough, my friend.

Outside the palace stretches a park, wide and welcoming, where you'll find a scattering of benches beneath a canopy of ancient trees. One month into my study abroad journey, I was sitting there journaling when I was struck by a revelation—the answer to the question I'd been asking since I arrived.

I realized I was exactly the same person in Belgium as I was back home in California.

I'm not sure what I thought was going to happen. I hadn't expected an international Jekyll-and-Hyde experience, so to speak, but I *had* wondered whether my actions and beliefs and ways of being were simply confirmations of the social feedback loops around me.

But here, in a different country, on a different continent, surrounded by students and coworkers and a family and a culture that spoke and thought and interacted differently than I did, I realized I was still just *me*. I was still the girl who stayed up too late and drank too much coffee and sang just a little off-key. I still tried too hard and loved too much and didn't feel the need to do anything because the other kids were doing it. I still loved meeting new people and sketching new landscapes and believed the world could be a little better than it was.

Sitting there on that park bench, I realized I still thought and valued and believed all I had before, but now I knew those values were my own. I wasn't a product of my environment, although it had enabled me to know more of who I was.

I had to go halfway around the world to find myself, and here I was. The same girl I'd known in California, only a little wiser, probably, for having ventured so far beyond my comfort zone. I sighed in relief at the revelation, then went off to find a chocolate shop.

The Slump

I sensed a lot of discouragement in your letter this month, Ash, as much as you talked about what's next. I wonder if you're not a bit anxious to be onto the next big thing.

This is a season for dreaming: about the great adventures you want to embark on in college, and how you hope to spend these years, and even what you will do afterward. But it's also a difficult time for most students because, after the newness and excitement of freshman year has waned, drudgery sets in. There's a reason they call it *the sophomore slump.*

Ash, I hear you when you say you're burned out and tired. Exhausted, probably. School is so much better yet so much harder than you imagined, and at times it feels like your motivation is running dry.

First, I want to reaffirm how proud I am of you: for taking the honors classes, for adding the extracurriculars, and for choosing the harder professors so you'll learn even more than you have to. So much of what we take out of school is a mathematics game, an exponent of what we put in. I'm convinced the more you apply your talents in this season—sounding mentorly yet?—the more you'll reap in the days and years to come.

I also understand this slump you're feeling. What once seemed novel about school has become wholly mundane. College life is finally your new normal, and there's not much thrilling in normal. There is a lot of life that can feel like this, actually. The thud of the day after day is as familiar as the drip of a faucet or the tick of a grandfather clock.

What makes someone special is not their ability to escape the limits of everyday life, but rather their capacity to expand within them. To find wonder and adventure and magic in the midst of normalcy. We don't need to travel overseas to explore a new world because there are worlds to explore all around us. Have you hiked the mountains behind the college at night? Have you painted a picture of the sky outside your window? Have you met an exchange student and learned phrases in her language or tasted her favorite foods? There are worlds within our world if we would only be curious enough to explore them. Like the way I felt the first time friends took me to the end of San Ysidro Lane, a place I'd driven past a hundred times on the highway. If you make a right through the bushes at the very end and walk along the shrouded path, it spills out along a channel where you can go over a walking bridge and onto Hidden Beach. I'll take you sometime to explore there.

As the artist Andy Warhol said, "You need to let the little things that would ordinarily bore you suddenly thrill you."[1] Doing so is counter to our culture of entertainment and newness and next. Learning to magnify your world is one of the most pure and profound practices you can cultivate.

Counting

Even though I know the value of seeing the exciting amid the ordinary, sometimes I still have such a propensity to go looking for adventure that I miss the wild absurdities happening right in front of me. Even when I'm overseas.

On one of those last December walks in the Belgian forest,

the trees barren and tall and tangled, Clementine laughed about the boy at a recent birthday party who, in broken English, had called me "the beautiful American." Mind you, I think it was tongue-in-cheek, because I'd used the wrong converters and blown out the fuses at the house and my straightener wasn't working and I was looking notably frizzy and unkempt. Clem made a reference to him being a prince.

"Huh?" I said, looking at her sideways. "Wait, why was there a prince at your friend's birthday party?"

"Oh," she said nonchalantly. "Well, because my friend is a countess."

The pieces started coming together then, Ash, like slow-motion evidence shots in a tacky TV drama. I remembered the invitations from other royal families. I pictured the signed boyhood picture of a Belgian king, sitting without fanfare on the old wooden desk in my room—beside the giant armoire and clunky radiator with the little mouse I'd named Mortimer who lived underneath.

"Clem," I said slowly, "why do you have friends who are countesses? And why do you and your sisters get invitations to big international parties hosted by royal families from other countries?"

"Well!" She turned to me, speaking quickly and matter-of-factly now. "I am a countess too. All three of us are. Because my father is a count, and his father was a count, and he was given that title by the king."

I must have looked surprised, because she added, "Honestly, Allison, everyone is royalty here."

Ah yes, I thought. *Just like America.*

Sometimes we're so caught up in our own small realities that we fail to see the bigger story. Or, you know, the fact that our sweet and unassuming host father is a count, like the one from Monte Cristo.

Souvenirs

Europe, Ash, was a sensory overload of grand architecture and crusty hostels and a hundred new landscapes. I spent a strange Thanksgiving in Serbia, exciting weekends in Paris and Prague, and crossed the UN green zone into the Turkish Republic of Northern Cyprus.

On trains and in hostels along the way, I met travelers who'd commemorated their journeys with small flag patches pinned like tiny trophies on their backpacks. Each pin purchased at a gift shop in their country of representation, and ironically made in China. I wanted some. A collection, that is, even though I didn't have a backpack.

I think this idea occurred to me on an Irish Duck tour half-way through my time abroad, and I sat for a while wondering how I could make up for the countries I'd already visited. Could I go back? Or buy the pins all at once in a multinational gift shop? I reasoned it would be okay because I technically *had* just been to those countries, and the flags are made in China, anyway.

Eventually I settled for postcards, then nothing at all. Because I realized all my fretting over souvenir purchasing actually meant I was missing the view from the bell tower that day. Instead, I gathered mementos as one makes new friends: naturally, serendipitously, with meaning and sweet memories.

Ash, when we live as if we only care about goals and achievements and finish lines, it is like traveling for the mere purpose of collecting cheap trinkets to show off to friends.

Besides, no one actually wants to see your souvenirs, I've learned. They want to hear your stories. Especially the ones where everything went horrifically wrong and you were stranded on a Norwegian sailboat in Ireland watching the sunrise from the deck.

I'll tell you that one someday.

Oh the Places

Wherever you go, however much you travel, never lose your wonder for the world, Ash.

The wanderlust for the horizon is a thirst that we quench again and again, and never stop quenching. The very thirst means we're alive, in the way we don't satisfy our body's need for hydration with a single drink of water. Adventure is equal parts beautiful and terrifying, and you will know yourself better when you brave it.

I'm excited for wherever the journey takes you, but I do think Italy is a spectacular choice. As Dr. Seuss said, "Oh, the places you'll go."[2]

But wherever you go, Ash, wherever your wanderlust takes you, promise me you'll never wear socks to a formal luncheon. Even if they're argyle.

Ciao!

X A

> People travel to wonder
> at the height of the mountains,
> at the huge waves of the seas,
> at the long course of the rivers,
> at the vast compass of the ocean,
> at the circular motion of the stars,
> and yet they pass by themselves
> without wondering.
>
> ST. AUGUSTINE

CHAPTER 11

ON DESIRE & SERVING

If we have no peace, it is because we've
forgotten that we belong to each other.

MOTHER TERESA

MAY 13

Ash,

Happy birthday, beautiful!

Well, birthday month, at least. I'm a firm believer in celebrating birthday weeks on a normal year, and birthday months for a new decade, or significant birthdays, or golden birthdays. Christie celebrates half birthdays, too, and justifies many gifts to herself that way. But this is a full birthday month for you, Ash, and twenty is no small feat. You're no longer a teen!

I've been in Ireland for Aoife's wedding this week. The Irish don't just host weddings; they host three-day *céilidhs*, where singing and dancing abound. I'm staying with Laura in her family home at Westport, set amid sprawling green hills and sheep-speckled pastures and ancient stone pubs with red doors. It's the sort of setting I'd want for a children's book that contained only pictures. We came here after the wedding and decided we ought to go for a walk along the cliffs above the ocean, and since we were above the ocean, we thought we might as well jump in.

We climbed over fences and hiked through fields dusted with cotton and came to the edge of the Emerald Isle, where Laura belted Gaelic folk songs out across the Atlantic. Between the grey sky and greenery, Ireland is freezing in May. We stripped down to our swimsuits and pale, shivering knees and then jumped, laughing hard and terrified, into the thrashing ocean. It took me two seconds to scream, the water both freezing my bones and searing the magic of the moment into my story.

I've learned that sometimes in life you just have to jump in. Nothing in my mind wanted my body to hit that ocean, and everything in my heart knew the ocean was where the memories were made.

Sometimes, you just need to jump in the ocean. No matter how cold.

The Tenderloin

Ash, I loved what you said in your last letter about wanting to impact your local community. You'll have to come with me to the Tenderloin next time you visit. You'd love this place instantly, although it took me a long time to jump into that ocean called serving.

When Jess first told me over omelets and orange juice at

Ella's in Lower Pacific Heights that she was volunteering at a homeless ministry in San Francisco, I did one of those saccharine smile-and-nods that may fool a stranger but looks totally fake to a friend. Jess would later work with me and become a very close friend herself, but thankfully we'd just met that morning, so she didn't sense my insincerity.

Don't get me wrong, Ash, I loved the idea of working with the homeless. But *I* just didn't want to be the one doing it. Maybe somewhere else, someday, but not in San Francisco. Not in the Tenderloin. Anywhere but the Tenderloin.

You see, I never wanted to come to this city in the first place, for several valid reasons. For one, I always get parking tickets when I have meetings in San Francisco. I once received three in one day, all within the same four blocks. And not a single ticket was for going over the two-hour limit. *(Street sweeping! Wheels not turned to the correct angle! Blocking one-quarter inch of an almost-faded crosswalk!)* When I pulled the third ticket off my windshield that afternoon, I was laughing like a clown in a fun house. I know the parking attendant was watching from somewhere behind a tree. Clearly San Francisco, with its steep streets and quaint trolley cars and zealous parking attendants, was *not* for me.

The real reason I didn't want to move to San Francisco ran deeper, though. I had spent a spring break in college working in the inner city, and I was scared of the hardship I saw there. It was not a great week. In fact, it was pretty depressing, even though I'd convinced myself that bringing groceries to shut-ins made me a holier person than my peers who were bringing surfboards to the beach.

At the end of that summer I drove my brother the two hours north from Santa Cruz to find him new clothes for the school year. We couldn't fathom the thought of paying fifteen dollars for a parking spot near downtown, so we drove a few blocks south into the Tenderloin. The neighborhood looked sketchy, sure, but the parking lots were a fraction of the price! What were a few extra blocks if it meant saving ten bucks? We pulled right in.

Walking back to the car as evening fell, we passed by a large group of people on the sidewalk, all intoxicated and raucous. We sped up our pace as they laughed and jeered and catcalled me. Then a man grabbed me from behind, right on my butt. I gasped, staggering for a moment in shock.

Adam spun around. "Hey!" he exclaimed, moving forward to confront the man.

"It's okay, it's okay!" I hushed my brother, pushing him forward. We had to leave. I knew we weren't safe.

I could still feel the man's hand on me as we sped away that night, like the burn on fresh-branded cattle. I never wanted to live in San Francisco.

Ever.

That's why I didn't want to hear about Jess's wonderful work with the homeless in the Tenderloin—because now that I had moved to SF, I knew that I needed to go. Facing that inner-city place meant facing my inner-city fears, and I didn't know if I was ready.

But go I did.

I think what eventually brought me there was the disconnect I was starting to feel in my own daily grind. I spent six days a week working on behalf of trafficking survivors, but I did so from behind a shiny MacBook in cafés with four-dollar lattes and colleagues who dressed just like me. I could talk about pain and poverty and oppression and hardship, and I could work on behalf of its alleviation, but I wasn't touching it. I wasn't letting it touch me.

The first few times I went to City Impact with Jess, I needed the people being served more than they needed me. I don't mean that in some lofty, spiritual sense. I mean it in the realm of social anxiety. The Tenderloin residents knew one another, and I knew no one. They were the tribe, and I was the outsider who so badly wanted to feel accepted. Isn't it the simplest human desire to want to fit in?

The organization had been doing this work for three decades, meeting peoples' needs hand-to-hand, seven days a week. The more I went, the more I wanted to go back, until I was spending most Sunday afternoons there after church. I not only loved it but made friends. I heard their stories; I learned about their trials and addictions and abusive pasts. I visited the apartments of the people who had homes. I smelled the stenches and ate the food and prayed the prayers they needed. I asked them to pray for me.

I didn't love San Francisco until I fell in love with its inner city.

Blessed to Be

When I was in Jordan, we visited the Dead Sea, a must for any American passing through the Middle East. You really do *float* too. You wander in and tip onto your back, and up you go! Feet out of water. The salt stings every crevice of your body as blobs of dark mud cover you from the shore. It's surreal. It's also a great exfoliating treatment.

Do you know why the Dead Sea is dead, Ash? It's not just a name. The Dead Sea truly is dead. A liquid pool of salt, it has no life in it whatsoever. But contrary to popular thought, the sea isn't dead because nothing flows into it. In fact, the Jordan, the most holy of rivers, is one of its main waterways. The Dead Sea is dead because nothing flows *out* of it. It has no life because it's all input, no output.

My pastor, Britt, likens this to our spiritual lives sometimes.

We pour in, pour in, pour in: books, lectures, podcasts, conferences. For the pious, add in daily Bible readings, prayer sessions, small groups. And yet, I have often found that despite being flooded with religiosity, I can feel spiritually vacant after all of these inputs. I continue to fill my life with spiritual and emotional and intellectual good, yet I feel a bit . . . dead.

The truth is, we need both input *and* output in order to have life. Water must flow in, but water must also flow out.

There's a beautiful passage in the Hebrew scriptures where God is speaking to Abraham in Genesis, spelling out the nature of his relationship with the Jewish people. In short, he says they are blessed to be a blessing.

What a simple, beautiful truth. We, you and I, Ash, are blessed that we might bless others. All of these gifts, opportunities, relationships, abilities, and experiences—they're all blessings, that we might bless others through them. We lead privileged lives here in this part of the world. We're of a generation where everything is available to us, all knowledge just a click away. Yet, largely speaking, we feel more disconnected to one another than our neighbors in developing nations.

I'd argue this feeling exists because we actually *are* more disconnected. We're disconnected from the pouring out because we've been so consumed by the pouring in, thinking we can never get enough.

My friend and spiritual hero, Bob, became so exasperated by this trend in our society that one day he just up and quit Bible studies. Instead, he meets regularly with a group of men for Bible *doings*. They just go out and find ways to "do" their faith together.

Ash, I've watched you mature so much in this season. You have gained so much wisdom and insight. What now, my dear girl, will you go out and do?

Original Sin

When it comes to doing faith, I'm learning every day and I've always been painfully imperfect. I still remember my first sin— okay, I'll call it what it is: *my first crime*—like it was yesterday. I'm haunted with guilt even now. Just a twinge.

I was playing at my friend Katie's house on the other side of town. She was boisterous and sweet and had an amazing toy collection. Shelves and shelves of toys, higher than you could reach. And her mom made us microwave lunches with mac and cheese and mushy apple-cinnamon sauce that had dancing penguins on the outside of the box.

Did I mention I was three? Like I said: *first* sin. But I feel like it was yesterday.

After lunch Katie and I went back upstairs to play with her wondrous toy collection—specifically, her Barbie dolls. My favorite. I loved the outfits and dresses and make-believe lives we could invent for them. I've always said my favorite childhood activity was dress-up, and not much has changed to this day.

I had just dressed one of these buxom Barbies when, like a cop showing up at a college party, my mom arrived downstairs. Katie, the angel child she was, went running down to greet her, but I panicked, frozen. I didn't want to leave! How could this perfect day end?

That's when it happened.

My mind could not control my body. I reached for one flawless Barbie shoe on the shelf, and I took it. *Snatched it.* Put it into my pocket. A miniature high heel in my favorite color— aqua. It was oh so glamorous, and I didn't have any Barbie shoes like it. God knows what I expected to do with *one* Barbie shoe. I just wanted to preserve that perfect playdate somehow.

A moment later my mom was on the stairs, collecting me and waving good-bye and strapping me into my car seat. The shoe burned a hole in my pocket and my conscience. I could barely speak as she asked me questions about my day. I was too wracked with guilt over what had transpired.

For years, maybe decades, I carried the secret with me, Ash. And that Barbie shoe. I know: *ridiculous.* But in the mind of a three-year-old, I had committed the ultimate betrayal.

Perhaps this is why I accepted Jesus into my heart at such a young age. Years ahead of my peers, I knew what it meant to repent.

All-Consuming

I saw a neon sign recently that said, *All I ever wanted was everything.*

That's my life most days, Ash. I want everything. I'm a victim of our culture of never enough. It's crazy to think that an item will make me happy. Insane, really. To think a new piece of clothing, or the month's hottest gadget, or the *Autumn Auburn* makeup palette will dramatically improve my quality of life. They say money can't buy happiness, yet every time, I think it will! It *never* does.

Where does this sensation come from?

I've processed the question over and over again—usually while nursing blisters from the new pair of heels that I cannot return and have committed to never, ever wearing again. I can't speak for other shopaholics or the average partaker in consumer therapy, but for me, I think it's a deep-seated desire to be made new. I want to feel remade, reimagined, reborn. I want to feel like I'm progressing, advancing—still myself, but an updated version. Allie 2.0.

So, I buy new things.

The problem is, new things never make me new. Sure, there is an initial, addictive rush of dopamine to the brain. The chemical cleanse that makes our eyes open wide in delight and then narrow in a possessive gaze. "That *will* be mine." A familiar flash of Gollum-esque desire for the ring. Then there's the satisfaction of the purchase. And oh, is it satisfying! Opening the box, or putting it on, or taking it out for a spin. Sometimes the joy is sustained, often in proportion to how long I've wanted the thing, or how much I've saved and sacrificed for it. Anticipation that's built from how much it cost me.

Yet every time, sooner or later, it's the same effect. The sugar rush of greedy need slumps into listless boredom. The newness wears off, and I'm back to being me. Only with a few more things.

Then inevitably, the hour comes when I set my eyes on something else I want. *This time*, I think, *this thing will make me new.*

The Longing

When I was six years old and long repentant of my kleptomaniac ways, I received a catalog in the mail from a new company selling dolls called *American Girl*. I was enchanted. Enraptured.

I determined that Felicity, the redheaded colonial child who loved horses, ball gowns, and adventure was my alter ego in figurine form. Boy, did I want her. Not just any American Girl doll, but *her*—because the connection was personal. The company, brilliantly, had included a two-page life-size spread of each doll. I would lie on my bed and stare at her image by nightlight, imagining what it would be like to have her with me in the flesh. I mean, plastic. I already felt like she was mine.

For two years and several centuries I wanted that doll until one day, after a show of childhood character I'll tell you about another time, my parents sat me down and told me I would be getting Felicity. Not *a* Felicity, but *my* Felicity. *Overjoyed* is too light a word to describe how I felt. She arrived, and she was wonderful, and I still have her to this day ready to hand down to my little girl, should God ever entrust me with one.

But the point is, Ash, what I eventually realized was that I would never feel the same level of enraptured desire for the doll as when I *didn't* have her. When I wanted her. I wonder if the greatest joys in life aren't often found in sheer anticipation. In the waiting and the wanting and the dreaming and the desire.

I believe we're designed for desire in the same way we're designed to crave warmth, or sleep, or food, or love. All these desires point us to something beyond, to something greater. Our lives are not made for immediate gratification. The best things often happen when we live within the tension of desire and don't always rush to satiate it. We must learn to enjoy the longing, for in the longing is joy itself.

I think our culture has lied to us a little. All of our advertising and media tells us day after day that a life well lived is a constant satiation of longing. If that is the case, then why do I know of so many wealthy and famous people who are dissatisfied? Thriving is learning to live with an ache that can't be filled, but must be felt. There is goodness found and character grown when we sit in the waiting and longing and allow it to refine us like a fire scorching silver, burning away everything that's not precious metal. Those who always rush to satisfy their wants never enjoy the painful brilliance of this process. They never experience the truer joy of a great longing satisfied on the other side of long-suffering patience.

Why is romance so sweet at its outset? Because it's brimming full of newness, running over with yearning, and held in the glorious tension of desires yet to be fulfilled.

The longing is what we're all longing for.

Still Haven't Found

I think our culture tells us all our desires can be fulfilled, and it breeds disenchantment and depression when we can't get no satisfaction. Then again, I think religion sometimes does this too.

Do you know the song "I Still Haven't Found What I'm Looking For" by U2? It's one of my favorites. I was thrilled one day in high school when the worship leader began playing it on Sunday morning.

I crooned alongside my girlfriends, repeating the familiar chords again and again and thinking how hip we all were to be singing U2 at church. Until we hit the last verse, and the worship leader added his own ending: "Now I've finally found what I'm looking for!" he belted with a smile, strumming triumphantly on the guitar strings.

I frowned.

I wasn't unhappy because he'd changed the song. I was frowning because I felt like his change missed the point.

"If I find in myself a desire which no experience in this world can satisfy," said C. S. Lewis, "the most probable explanation is that I was made for another world."[1]

We have to lean into the longing, Ash. We're not meant to just arrive. The appetite for something more points us to something beyond what we can consume or grasp.

Pursuits

On the matter of more practical longings, in your last letter you asked if I thought you should go for that competitive internship next year. I know it would take a lot of commitment and work on your part to get it. My answer to this, and to any question of pursuits like it, will almost always be, "Yes! If . . ."

Yes, if you want it, and if it makes you light up inside, and if you feel like you've got a good shot, then yes, yes, yes. Of course, my dear! You ought to go for it.

But most important: yes, if your identity is not tied to it. This will take some deep self-reflection on your part. Do not pursue it, as wonderful as it is, if you will be crushed and your world will fall apart if you *don't* get it. I say this not because I'm afraid of your disappointment in that event. You'd eventually be fine. I say it because I would worry for you in success.

If you want something so badly that your whole identity surrenders to it, imagine the manic, obsessive person you would become if you got it. Never go after something that's become an idol. Something that, once you have it, will wrap its inky tentacles around your heart and not let you remember yourself apart from it.

The Oscar winners we love the most are the ones who worked the hardest but never expected to win the little gold statue. Their joy was in the process, in the journey of their work, and not in the accolades at the end. My friend Pamela, who followed in her father's footsteps in the acting world, told me once that the best actors love the auditions. They don't live for getting the part. Practicing and auditioning and getting rejected are all part of the journey they enjoy and embrace.

We love the actors who recognize an Academy Award for what it is: a little gold statue. And who trip going up the stairs to accept it.

Character

Ash, I just want to say how much I admire your heart. The way you love and serve and honor people, even when no one is looking. It convicts and inspires me.

Like last weekend at Perry's wedding, I saw you spend half the reception talking to the old man working at the coat check. You gave him as much attention, courtesy, and respect as you did the CEO of a billion-dollar company. To me, that isn't just kindness—it's character. It's why you're so beautiful to people. It's the inner light that illuminates your outer being and draws people in.

Character, I've heard it said, is how you treat those who can do nothing for you.[2] You are not afraid to shine some light on the dark predispositions we have about people who are different from us. It's one of the things we all admire most about you, Ash.

Keep me posted on the internship.

I'm proud of you,

PS—I still have that Barbie shoe.

A religion true to its nature must also be concerned about man's social conditions. . . . Any religion that professes to be concerned with the souls of men and is not concerned with the slums that damn them, the economic conditions that strangle them, and the social conditions that cripple them, is a spiritually moribund religion.

MARTIN LUTHER KING JR.

CHAPTER 12

ON WONDER & BELIEVING

Some things have to be believed to be seen.

MADELEINE L'ENGLE

JULY 9

Dear Ash,

I loved my days in Haiti.

Warm afternoons in the nape of a hammock, toes dug into the sand beneath palm trees and coconuts, rocking slowly from side to side. From there the world was magnified. Children played football on the beach, their laughter echoing beyond the chain-link fence that divided our Western world from theirs.

Guards patrolled the boundary of the disaster-assistance outpost, guns slung back like toys. If I smiled at them, they'd ask, *"Sec Passe?"* Creole's French-like version of "How's it going?" My joy was to chant back, *"Nou ap boule!"* to which they'd bust up with delight. "We're burning!"—a favorite Haitian phrase.

Haiti was harsh. It's the poorest country in the Western hemisphere, devastated by the recent earthquake and still in a communal state of aftershock. Accompanied by armed guards on motorbikes, we journeyed into Cité Soleil, the poorest, most

Seeing my brother living out his calling in Haiti. I've never been more proud.

dangerous city, and spent time with the community and doctors serving in the clinics there.

I came to Haiti to visit my brother, Adam, who arrived as an aid worker with Samaritan's Purse just months after the earthquake hit and days after his college graduation. He has been there ever since, now monitoring the impact of emergency relief. I've never been more proud of him.

When the world looks at Haiti now, it just sees devastation. But the people, the culture, and the country itself are beautiful. Magical, actually, and I loved it more than I knew I could love a place. We walked with locals on the beach, got stung by tiny jellyfish swimming to an island in the sea, and danced to Rihanna on a helipad at night with dozens of kids from the community.

I've never been to a better dance party.

The Plague

When it comes to memories, we carry all kinds. Some, like Haiti, are gifts to be treasured for a lifetime, while others are more like the discount holiday sweaters from Great-Aunt Greta that you feel obliged to wear when she's in town.

Middle school memories are the latter for me. I wish I could forget them as easily as I forget people's names or the place where I last left my house keys. Were those good years for you? That season was pretty awful for me. I mean, really awful. Seventh grade specifically.

The first two weeks went fine. Sure, I felt awkward in my own skin, but I had some friends and liked my classes and was tepidly optimistic about the future.

Okay! I thought. *I can do this seventh-grade thing.*

Until that fateful day, three weeks in, when Corey—with whom I'd spent the summer—decided she no longer liked me. To this day, I don't know why. Maybe it's because I wasn't athletic and had worn braces for too many years. Or maybe it was because my clothes were oversized department-store knockoffs and my bushy bangs sat like an awkward visor across my pimpled face. Whatever the reason, logical or not, overnight Corey went from being one of my best friends in the world to avoiding me like the plague.

Because it was middle school, the other girls followed. No one wants the plague.

There are few things more terrifying than eating lunch alone on the bench every day in seventh grade. If I tried to join my group of former friends, no one would talk to me. I wondered if people could see me. Was I that bad?

I hated getting to school early because everyone would stand in clusters across the quad: the cool girls, the semi-cool girls, the partiers, the skater guys, the jocks. I would float, awkwardly, among them. My heart would start thudding; my hands would sweat and hang awkwardly at my sides. I would pull them into my sweatshirt pocket and lift the grey hood over my ears, doing a loop in search of a lone friendly face or any welcome glance. Then I'd hurry back to my locker once more, pretending I'd forgotten something I knew I already had.

Just look busy, I thought. *Just survive.*

When I remember the moments of my life, I think in terms of snapshots, like photos in a frame. But I don't want to frame any middle school pictures. My standout shots are moments I'd rather forget, like getting pooped on by seagulls, or scolded by teachers for running to the lunch line, or laughed at by eighth graders when my backpack zipper broke as I rushed to the bus. The eighty-seven textbooks I carried spilled across the ground, and the girls' pretty faces cackled as I scrambled and fumbled, mortified, to pick everything up. I walked at a backward slant all those years from the weight of both my books and my anxieties. Every now and then one of the popular girls would call me after school, and I would be elated—even though it was just for homework help. Being needed by someone could carry me to the end of the week.

Seventh-grade yearbook. That's me in all my glory.

My ten-year-old brother got sick that fall. Extremely sick. My mom drove him back and forth to doctors and specialists trying to find someone who could help him. He missed nine weeks of school as he was turned away again and again, his small body wasting away. "Maybe it's just emotional," the specialists offered. "Maybe he doesn't like his teacher."

No one knew what was causing Adam's illness, but he grew paler and thinner and weaker by the day. I watched my parents' distress and went silent—making it my goal to do well in school and not be a problem. I hurt for my family, and I didn't want to be any cause for further distress. I didn't want to be seen.

I was scared: for my brother, for my family, for myself. And when I get scared, I turn inward. I was twelve, and I had no idea who or how to ask for help.

Promises to God

In a strange way, Ash, I found a faith of my own that seventh-grade year.

I was by myself so much, and so socially petrified, that I would pray, and pray, and pray. I think God met me there, as he always does in our sufferings, tiny or great. I made a twelve-year-old promise then that I would never forget how my isolation felt. I told God that one day, when I wasn't the outsider, I would carry that empathy with me and love people better than I was being loved at the time.

Looking back, I think that's pretty profound thinking for a preteen.

Or maybe I was just desperate.

Either way, I will never forget one bright spring afternoon during lunch hour. I had somehow managed to stand in the outer ring of the cluster of semi-cool girls and was feeling grateful for each sacred moment. For once, I was not alone. Until someone in the inner ring suggested they go somewhere, and the herd began to move like bison on a plain. I hesitated, frozen, as my hope slipped away on the blacktop. When the herd leaves a bison, the lions come out.

Suddenly my new friend from science class, Stephanie, turned around to catch my gaze. "Allie!" she called, motioning with her hand as they walked away. "Come with us."

I leaped forward, vowing before heaven and earth in that moment I would never forget her kindness. Her simple act of inclusion meant more to me than she would ever know.

Adam's health returned that spring too. A small miracle, by all counts.

He joined me in middle school the following year as a sixth grader. On the rare and beautiful days that I found a group to sit with, he would hide behind trash cans and pelt Goldfish crackers at me and my fragile social position. I was embarrassed, but grateful. I was not alone, and I still had a brother, as annoying as he was.

Last Pick

Dear friend, to this day, I still cringe when I drive past my middle school. Perhaps that makes me petty, because we were so young and it was so long ago and I should probably be mature and totally over it by now. I'm a grown-up, for goodness' sake. I've done something with my life! But a scattering of raw emotions still blows across that blacktop, like the paper bags and tinfoil left behind after lunch hour.

And yet—I know that place played a role in making me *me*.

That season taught me to care for the left out and the lonely and the forgotten and the last. Because I was, quite literally, the girl chosen last. I would stand on the field as the cool kids picked their teams, feeling as wanted as an unmatched sock at the bottom of the laundry bin. Their faces labored over who, between the remaining two of us, was the best worst choice, and I wondered why this iconic moment, depicted in every schoolyard cartoon and Little-League drama, was my life in living color.

Being the outsider cracked the soil of my soul, and into those deep crevices I felt God pouring the fertile seeds of empathy. One day those seeds would blossom into greater faith—a faith put into practice as I learned to love others in the ways I wanted to be loved.

A faith for the last and the least.

A faith for people like me.

Where It Becomes Real

Ash, can we talk about faith? You've spoken of it less lately, and I think I might know why. I wonder if God has not been the God you thought he was lately. Do you feel, perhaps, as if he's let you down somehow? I could understand why you would.

The pain your friend is going through, the global poverty you've begun to engage, the messiness of church history, your questions about the Scriptures. The things you once enjoyed making sense of don't seem to make much sense anymore. Maybe it feels like God isn't answering your phone calls. You dial and wait, but the line just keeps ringing.

I've had seasons of doubt too, and will most certainly have more. Long, arduous months of feeling as if my God, who was once so dependable, has stood me up at the dining table of hard questions, alone and waiting for the bill.

But this, sweet Ash, is where we lean in. This is where faith becomes real.

The Glow Stars

When I was a little girl, I loved to lie in bed at night and stare at the glow stars on my ceiling. They were wondrous and near and luminous and certain. I could count them, every one. They taught me to look up and then keep looking, to search for their forms in the dim of the night as they lit something up in my heart.

I loved my glow stars.

Then one night something happened. Maybe the sky was especially clear or the air was unusually still or the light of the moon was particularly bright. But that evening something changed as I stood outdoors and gazed up: the brilliance of the constellations, dazzling and infinite, *captivated* me.

You see, I'd known the stars were always there, of course, but I'd never comprehended them. Maybe I wasn't ready to. They were too far away in their burning, too limitless in their number, too beyond my time and place to understand. I've heard there are ten thousand stars for every grain of sand. My glow stars, on the other hand, were right above my bed. I could jump on my mattress and reach up and touch them, nearly. Their imitation was enough for me—until one night it wasn't.

On that night, I became enchanted. I stood in dewy grass taking in the constellations with new eyes, enraptured and awed and uneasy. Overwhelmed by just how small I was and how little I knew of the greatness beyond. It was frightening and compelling, and I could not get enough of this new wonder raging in my soul.

"There is something beautiful about a billion stars held steady by a God who knows what He is doing," said Donald Miller. "They hang there, the stars, like notes on a page of music, free-form verse, silent mysteries swirling in the blue like jazz."[1]

After that night, and every night stargazing since, I was never again satisfied with my glow stars.

The Wrestling

There was a point, Ash, when I'd really made sense of my faith. It was big, but I had my arms around it. I wouldn't have traded that near and familiar faith for the world.

Until I began to ask better questions, harder questions. And I was presented with the same choice I'd had as a child: to stare at the certainty of my glow stars, or to wander beneath the magnitude of the night. To be brave enough to realize that my imitation stars were always meant to point me toward a greater truth. In the way a postcard from Tanzania might inspire wanderlust but will never rival standing at the top of Mount Kilimanjaro.

I had the option, then, of staying beneath what I could wrap my mind around or journeying into the mystery of what I could never fully know. Because the more I come to contemplate the universe today—its light-years and galaxies and dark matter and supernovas—the less I understand it. It's only when I'm willing to risk not comprehending that I can grow in my capacity for wonder and awe and wild goodness.

In the Hebrew Scriptures there is a section of books called the Talmud that isn't included in the Old Testament Bible. The books were written much later than the other Judeo-Christian texts and are canonized in Judaism. Essentially, they are varying perspectives of different rabbis debating the meaning of the sacred texts.

The Jewish people canonized the debate because they believed God is found in the wrestling.

We need strong frameworks of faith to hang the flesh of our beliefs on, Ash. But we must also trust that the messy, dark place of hard questions is the very marrow inside the bones of belief. The inner place of uncertainty is where the stem cells of our beings grow. Life itself throbs in the marrow, bursting forth and allowing the whole body to thrive.

Just maybe, Ash, God isn't leaving our calls unanswered.

Maybe he was with us when we picked up the phone, when we had the thought to dial, when we experienced our moment of grief. Maybe God is in the call itself. Maybe he is the answer and the question, the celebration we sing and the cry that we sob, all the same. Maybe he really is Emmanuel, *God with us*—in all, and through all, and before all things.[2]

The Wind

Haiti was wrought with hard questions for me. Why must there be poverty, natural disasters, and suffering? Why is my life so charmed and comfortable compared to so much of the world? And how, in the midst of immense hardship, can people exhibit such insatiable, resilient joy? I asked many hard questions that trip, Ash. And then, when I couldn't wonder anymore, I turned my heart toward wonder.

I will never forget one of my last nights in Haiti, standing under the stars at night, wrapped in the warm breeze blowing over the water and through the trees, enveloping me.

There is something in warm wind that reaches the deepest parts of my spirit, Ash. That catches my breath as it sweeps through my hair and wraps around my shoulders. I don't feel this in cold wind. When it bites, I run indoors. But when the warm wind beckons, I open my arms.

In Santa Barbara there's a special type of wind that blows called the Santa Anas. The locals know it when it comes, rustling through the sycamore trees as it finds its way to the town. Warm, vivid gusts rushing through the streets as silver leaves whisper rhythmic tones in response.

When the Santa Ana winds blow, something in me lets go. That same childhood wonder I felt beneath the stars comes to life. Those nights I would roll down my windows and drive through the hills until I was lost. I would pray and cry and laugh and jump in Marge's pool and just sink. I would lie in the grass and stare at the shimmering sky and I'd listen to the wind.

Some people say they hear God's audible voice. I feel God's presence. I feel him stirring and speaking and directing in the warm wind—from Santa Barbara to Port-au-Prince.

And whenever I feel that wind blowing, I always smile and look up.

Here's to staring at the stars,

x A

My God, what is a heart,
That thou should'st it so eye,
And woo,
Powring upon it all thy art,
As if thou hadst nothing else to do?
GEORGE HERBERT

PART III

JUNIOR

CHAPTER 13

ON STYLE & COMMUNICATING

The traveler sees what he sees, the tourist
sees what he has come to see.

G. K. CHESTERTON

SEPTEMBER 31

Dear Ash,

What a thrilling experience you must be having. The art,
the architecture, the *spaghetti all'arrabiata*! I haven't heard from
you much, and I think that's a good thing. I would worry if you
were spending all your time in Italy writing letters to a pen pal.
You should be out in that great world exploring!

As George Bailey proclaims in *It's a Wonderful Life*: "Do
you know what the three most exciting sounds in the world
are? Anchor chains, plane motors, and train whistles." A journey
that involves all three? Well, dear girl, that's the very best kind
of adventure.

I loved the photos you sent. They reminded me of the week
I spent in Italy as a student: wandering the waterways of Venice,
the museums of Florence, the alleys of Siena, and the hills of
Tuscany. We took trains across the country and spent a day

and a half in Rome—which was far too short to see the sights, far too long to stay in our fifteen-euro hostel, and just enough time to determine it's one of my favorite cities in the world. In large part because a cup of gelato is more easy to come by than a bottle of water. My fellow students and I committed to trying a different scoop every day, twice a day, in every city, and to take a picture every time. The first photo we're exuberant; the fourth, still smiling; the tenth, looking grumpy and gorged.

Oh, Roma. Can you believe the magnitude of the Colosseum and the beauty of the piazzas? Watching history being unearthed beside you in open excavations along the public squares—it's mesmerizing. So often in America we forget the power of time and place. We don't live above a dozen layers of cities, where empires have risen and fallen, and will rise and fall again. These places tell our world's communal stories.

The Interviews

During my second week in Brussels, before my gelato journey, we had the opportunity to interview with a number of potential companies and NGOs for internship positions. Just like you did! There were several options that seemed interesting, but the one I really wanted was the position as a political *stagiaire* (fancy French word for "intern") at the European Parliament, in the office of a British Member of European Parliament (MEP).

I mean, what student studying the European Union in Brussels *wouldn't* relish an opportunity like that?

I was the third of three interviewees from our class and was uneasy about my chances. I'd gone through a few interviews already, traipsing back and forth across Brussels, getting lost on trams and buses in the scorching heat of early September. (These were the days before phones with Google Maps.) The first interview had left me inspired but confused about what the consultancy firm actually did. The next had been an international law firm working on an aspect of international law I knew nothing about, and the third, a small law firm, was so far outside town at the top of a steep hill that by the time I arrived, my black pantsuit was drenched in sweat and I was out of breath and panting. Pun not intended. It wasn't an elegant look.

Finally, my last interview: the European Parliament.

Emily, the MEP's political assistant, met me in the lobby. She was smart and bubbly and kind, with a pop of curly brown hair and an accent I could drum my fingers to like music. I wanted to work for Emily. She sped through the building with a skip in her step, showing me the ins and outs of this palace of political power. She even introduced me to Martin, the MEP himself.

I was offered the post shortly after and accepted with awed enthusiasm. One day, a few weeks in, I straight up asked her, "Why'd you choose me?"

Emily's desk was across from mine, and she barely glanced up to respond.

"Because of your handshake," she replied.

I was confused. She must have caught the furrow on my brow because she looked up over her monitor.

"You gave the best first impression," she said. "I could tell by your smile and demeanor in the first moments of meeting you that you were the type of person I wanted to work with. You were someone I wanted around the office. Because of that, you were the only one I introduced to Martin. I wouldn't have hired the others."

I learned that day, Ash, that there is little more memorable than a warm first impression.

My high school counselor, Mr. Pratt, taught us good handshakes when I was a junior. You link the web between your thumb and index finger with that of the person in front of you, grasp firmly (not too firmly!), and look them in the eye with a smile. Never again would I reach for someone's hand with my wrist bent awkwardly, as if handing them a tissue.

We'll practice your handshake next week when I see you.

The Message

Ash, you asked me recently for some practical advice to apply throughout your time studying abroad: your communicating, your writing, your internship. Your first foray into the professional world! What so few people realize, whether in class or the workplace or in social settings, is that we are all communicating all the time.

There's a communications theorist I studied in college named Marshall McLuhan. He's renowned in the field for his breakthrough thinking, backed by a catchy line he coined: "The medium is the message."

For decades, communications theorists only talked about the message itself—the words we said, or wrote, or conveyed otherwise. McLuhan was the first to argue that the very vehicle for carrying a message, be it a sticky note or a megaphone or a smoke signal, is a message in and of itself. The words *I love you* written by hand in a letter communicate something quite different when posted online in a tweet.

You and I are living vehicles for the messages we convey. From our gestures to our expressions to our outfits, the medium of our beings is constantly communicating. "I've learned," said the great Maya Angelou, "that people will forget what you said, people will forget what you did, but people will never forget how you made them feel."[1]

Imagine, Ash, that I'm standing on a podium and speaking for an hour, and you're listening somewhere in the audience. Now imagine someone asking you about the speech six months later. You'd probably recall the topic and one or two things I said, but more than anything, you'd remember how I made you feel—be it inspired, informed, discouraged, enraged, or totally lulled to sleep.

Many people think only of the words they are saying, rather than *how* their message is expressed. When it comes to short interactions, nothing will change the dynamic between two people more than a warm delivery and a smile.

Power Posers

While we're talking about presenting ourselves, have I shown you the power pose, Ash? If not, I will the next time I see you.

What we do with our bodies affects our minds and our spirits as much as it affects the people around us. There's a reason why we stand to show command and bow to show reverence. I recently attended a seminar where I learned the way we shape our bodies before we speak publicly or enter a meeting dramatically affects our energy and how people perceive us.

Thus, I give you *the power pose.*

A Deloitte study found that if you spread your arms wide and smile and laugh for three seconds before you walk onstage, you will come across as dramatically more confident, energetic, and likable.

The opposite is also true. If you curl up in a ball and frown, then speak moments later, your effect on people will adjust accordingly. Try it!

Dress to Impress

When I was fifteen I visited my cousins in Atlanta, and we strolled the cavernous corridors of a mall one afternoon to hide from the oppressive August heat. My older cousin, Rachel, was going on about how much she liked the clothes in Brooks Brothers, and I, of little fashion sense, was taking mental notes. I'd only recently decided that baggy T-shirts with stallion screen prints and knee-length jean-shorts weren't a flattering everyday look.

As we admired the luxurious fabrics in a window display, Rachel suddenly paused. "I love this," she mused, "but whatever I wear, the most important thing to me is looking approachable."

"What do you mean?" I implored. I couldn't imagine not wanting to dress in the prettiest clothes possible on *every* occasion.

"I mean, I always want to look nice," she said, "but I don't want to look so perfectly put-together that a random person on the street wouldn't feel like they can walk up and have a conversation with me." She shrugged. "I guess I just always want to be approachable."

I've never forgotten that moment, because it was the first time I realized what we wear communicates something. Think about the authority of a doctor's white lab coat, the seriousness of a business suit, or the fun of a flapper dress layered in fringe. It's the reason kids wear birthday crowns. Even when we're not speaking, our bodies and our gestures and our outfits speak for us.

When it comes to the clothes we choose, appropriateness also plays a big role. Shorts and a tank top may be nice for a walk on the beach, but they communicate the wrong message for a job interview. Likewise, if you wear a ball gown to sunbathe, you might get a few awkward glances.

My friend Jeannie believes in the impact of clothing so much that she made up a term for it: "wearapy." The very color of what we're wearing can bring energy and convey emotion. Think about how striking a red dress is, or an all-white outfit in the summer. Most people wear navy blue or black to a job interview. Jeannie says, wear yellow! A bright color communicates

Jeannie teaching me about "wearapy" during New York Fashion Week.

joy, positivity, verve. I don't own a lot of yellow, but I sure think I ought to.

Un Petit Peu

I learned a lot of British things at the European Parliament. Like how to make a proper cup of tea with Hobnobs, how to sign emails with an *x*—I still do that today—and how to *correctly* refer to many things ("Toss that in the rubbish" or "Let's take the lift!"). They also insist on adding an extra *u* to almost everything. Words like *colour* and *labour*. I'm still not sure why.

Language is a fascinating, funny thing when it traverses cultures—made all the harder when the languages themselves are different, as I learned with my francophone family. I knew only *un petit peu français*, and though my host sisters and mother were bilingual, my host father spoke almost no English. I attended dinners and events where everyone laughed and told stories in French, and I would nod along in earnest confusion. It was like trying to follow a sporting match without any idea of the rules or the teams or the point of the game. I never knew how challenging, frustrating, and humbling it could be to communicate. My cheeks would burn as I'd wrestle to say something I knew made no sense, and was so far from what I wanted to convey.

I never had much grace for people trying to speak another language until I struggled across a predominantly French and Flemish country, desperately trying to communicate.

There are few things I can recommend more than learning another language. And if you're going to spend extended time in any place, learning at least a little is a must. Even if you aren't confident in what you can say, always try to say something. The humbling, hilarious challenge of trying it alone will make you a better human.

Sticks and Stones

Speaking of words: Ash, I'm so sorry those things your manager said hurt your feelings. I'm sure she didn't mean that, but I can understand why you took it personally.

I've always heard it takes five compliments to balance out one negative comment, but in truth, I don't think it's such a simple equation. Words are powerful. They are like seeds scattered on the soil of our souls. Some blow away with the wind, but others put down roots. Some of those roots produce blossoms and fruit; others turn out to be kudzu weeds.

I'll never forget one sunny afternoon in first grade, sitting on a cinder-block planter with a group of other girls. One of them, whom I didn't know well but thought was really cool, suddenly turned and looked me square in the face. She analyzed my features.

"You're ugly!" she announced, her breath hot on my cheeks. Then she turned back to the group, as if she'd just made a comment about the weather.

I was ugly? *Wow,* I thought. *I didn't know I was ugly. Am I ugly?*

I was six years old, and she was six years old, and the comment was stupid and thoughtless and mean. But for whatever reason, those two words burrowed into my subconscious like a sand crab who never came out. Words have changed me too. In fifth grade some kids called me bossy, so I shut my mouth. I stopped trying to be a leader. I assumed leadership was not a desirable trait. I've since learned this happens to a lot of girls with big personalities, but I didn't know it then.

Those circumstances were so small, so incredibly insignificant, yet the words wrestled their way into the messages I told myself as I stared sullenly in the mirror for years onward. They are words I still hear. Growing up, we'd always chant: "Sticks and stones may break my bones, but words will never hurt me!" But that's not true, Ash. Words *can* hurt us. A lot.

Words don't just affect us in childhood. I once went on a date with a guy who made me feel insecure for being a "smart girl." Somehow, his one small comment rocked my confidence. I've realized since that I would rather be a "smart girl" spinster with swishy neon tracksuits and hanging plants and lots of cats than be with a man who made me feel insecure for being intelligent. No thanks.

All we can do when harsh or insensitive or thoughtless words fly at us—as they always, inevitably will—is to ground ourselves in the trueness of who we are. To believe a better story, and to give others grace even when they wound us. Hurt people hurt people, as the saying goes. If we don't know who we are, words can damage us deeply. But when we've internalized a healthy narrative about our identity, we can let those harsh words go. We can choose to find truth in honest critique and forgiveness in an uncalled-for affront. A chance to both forgive and remember how much our own words can impact another's life.

Gosh-Darned Nice

Words are powerful. We can wield them to hurt or to heal. We can use them to lambast or to give life, in both monumental ways and the smallest interactions.

Recently I was on a cross-country flight late in the evening and feeling extra chipper because I'd been given an upgrade, one benefit of frequently cramming myself into a tiny polyester seat at thirty thousand feet. I took notice of the steward tending our cabin. He was devoted to every guest, precise as he articulated his movements. Handing us hot towels with care, our bowls of nuts with flourish, my club soda and extra orange juice as if it were his utter delight.

He was quiet and gentle. Gracious. I saw his heart and his passion for his job. So I smiled and thanked him again and again. I wasn't overly appreciative. I just tried to meet his graciousness with gratitude, and my gratitude was sincere.

Toward the end of the flight, this sweet man slipped me a napkin with a note.

Thank you for being so gosh-darned kind and gracious! It read. *It was indeed a pleasure to serve you tonight. —Frank.*

Ash, never forget to appreciate people, and tell them as much. You do this so well already. Let's also remember to do our work like Frank, shall we? After eight hundred three-thousand-mile trips on an airliner from the mid-90s, I would probably lose my

My note from Frank, the precious flight attendant.

zeal. But Frank made that creaky cabin feel like the white linen dining hall at the top of the Eiffel Tower. He was totally present, and his care and consideration blessed the people he was serving. It blessed me.

On Writing

I'm so happy you're getting to write at this internship, and that you're loving it so much. After reading your letters every month, I daresay you have a talent for it.

It's beautiful that you're journaling too. Writing to share your story, and writing to better know your story. I think I like writing because it is so much like living well. You show up, you create, you risk something. You swim in it and suffer in it and are shaped by the very process of doing it. If you want to change lives, you get vulnerable, you get real. You make a mess, you are in process, you leave behind some things you love. Some sentences do not and will not ever fit.

In the end, good writing is like good people: wise and winsome and hilarious and true. Good writing makes you laugh out loud while it teaches you something profound. It draws you in and sparks something you didn't know could be kindled in your spirit. It makes connections; it opens doors. It acts with excellence and pours out its best, but never does it take itself too seriously. Great writing, like great friends, is worth keeping around.

Keep journaling and, at every turn, capturing this experience. Paint, write, sketch, photograph, or simply pause to sear the memory in your mind. Capture the color and emotion of seeing a new side of our world and watching the earth turn gold from this side of the sun. As Anne of Green Gables said, "I'm so glad I live in a world where there are Octobers."[2]

And all the more beautiful when those Octobers are in Europe.

Cheers—

x A

> That is part of the beauty of all literature. You
> discover that your longings are universal longings,
> that you're not lonely or isolated from anyone.
> You belong.
>
> F. SCOTT FITZGERALD

CHAPTER 14

ON ROMANCE & LEAVING

It is a truth universally acknowledged, that a single man in possession of a good fortune, must be in want of a wife.

JANE AUSTEN

NOVEMBER 29

Ash,

My dear girl, it was so good to hear your voice. I know Italy has been full of wild adventure but tempered with some painful regrets. That is so much of growing up, isn't it?

Mistakes will make every effort to seep into your identity, but do not let them. Of course it matters what you did, but what matters *most* is how you move forward from it. That is where the character of one's life is wrought. Guilt and shame will always try to meld mistakes into your identity. Hope and grace conspire to offer a better story.

There is an old African proverb that says, "Do not look where you fell, but where you slipped." Understanding where you slipped and why, and then making the decision in your spirit to turn from that way and not walk there again—that is wisdom, my dear. Very few people can admit their mistakes in the first place, and so they are controlled by their failings.

Our lives, darling girl, are not the sum of our failures, but the product of how we respond to them.

This Guy

You didn't say it on the phone, Ash, but I'm going to read between the lines. I wonder if this Italian guy you've started seeing is not the best influence on you? I'm hesitant to say much because I don't know him. And, of course, he sounds wonderful from the way you described him in your last note: intelligent and artistic, caring and charismatic. He's quite handsome too. I don't fault you for falling hard.

But I have to tell you, sweet Ash, you don't sound like yourself. You sound uncertain, uneasy. You don't have that spark of joy I'm so used to hearing in your voice. You talked less of other people and more about yourself. Which is fine, but it was in a way that sounded—how do I say this?—insecure. As if you're forgetting who you are.

I'm proud of you for asking hard questions about this relationship and where it's going. Preparing to come home in two weeks forces that decision, I suppose. Long-term logistics tend to pull at the cord of a relationship, either snapping the two parties closer or breaking them apart.

I can only imagine how difficult this decision must be for you, though. He's encouraging you to commit to long-distance before you come home, and you're wavering. That is a lot of pressure, and it can involve a great deal of pain too. You are right not to move forward until you have peace.

I know you feel alone in this choice, but I can empathize more than you know. I daresay I've found that journeying the difficult path of any hard decision is preferable to standing still at the fork in the road, knowing soon you must decide.

First Dates

I met DJ at church on a Sunday morning my senior year of college. I'd known who he was; everyone, it seemed, knew who the mildly famous, highly successful, college-dropout-turned-entrepreneur was. He had a house in the hills overlooking the ocean and a bevy of admirers and fans. He even had metal business cards, real metal business cards, with his silhouette carved in the middle. I was awed.

I think our first date was a Christian date. Meaning, he asked me to meet him at church and bring a DVD of the documentary I was working on so that if things got awkward, it was never really a date anyway. In case anyone asked.

I remember the service, but not the message. Sitting in my white jean skirt and tan-striped tank, August heat as heavy as a camping tarp on my shoulders. There I was, staring at my small pale legs next to his in the dark church hall, wondering if I should have worn such a short skirt to church, even in the oppressive heat.

What ensued was a whirlwind romance. It began with picnics between classes, and soon I was meeting his best friends. Bouquets of flowers and baskets of desserts landed at my apartment door. My roommates shared the sweets and giggled alongside me those weeks, waiting inside beneath the window when he'd walk me back from dinner. Listening in so they could gush with me and relive each detail, as good girlfriends do. Sure, we'd all gone on dates to formal dances and Rusty's Pizza Parlor with boys from our college courses. But DJ was different. He was classy, accomplished, established—a man. I think we all were romanced by the attention.

Things moved quickly those first months. We fought and broke up for five days over Thanksgiving and then were back together again and better than ever. I finished exams in political theory and ran outside to discover a Dom Perignon box perched on my windshield. One long-stemmed red rose was inside, along with a note saying my celebratory champagne was waiting at his house. I was standing on the pier with him one starry night that fall, looking out at the lights on the water, when he invited me to spend New Year's Eve with him and his friends.

On a private island. In Nicaragua.

The Island

I didn't say yes immediately. An international trip felt serious at twenty-one. What if it was perfect, but DJ and I didn't work out? I didn't want my life experience to peak too soon! But I did say yes, eventually. And promised myself I'd live many more epic experiences after, regardless.

The island was idyllic—the kind of place where the *Bachelor* finales are filmed. It was called Little Eden, a cloud of sand in the Pearl Cays. The villa where we stayed had been meticulously built through the years by a family from Europe who'd offered free use of the place to DJ's best friends. There were crystal chandeliers, long white couches, a shimmering pool, and a harp. Palm trees enshrouded the property on every side, and a small grey dock stretched out toward the sunset where bright blue sea kissed the shore.

Sure, it had been rough getting there. I forgot my passport, which turns out to be a not-so-minor detail when traveling internationally. That almost derailed the whole journey. After postponed flights and a frenzied search, we were off again. It was my first time flying first class—"the flossy," as the Black Eyed Peas would say. We took a prop plane from Managua to Bluefields, where we were delayed for the night by a tropical storm. I turned on the faucet in the hotel tub, and thick brown water poured from the spout. It reminded me of something Willy Wonka would have had in his factory, except it didn't smell like chocolate. I skipped the bath. The next morning we bounced violently for three and a half hours, sputtering over open ocean in a tiny boat steered by a local who sucked gasoline into his mouth and spat it into the engine.

The whole thing was odd and wild and worthy of reality television. A private chef from New Zealand joined us, diving for our dinner lobsters in the morning and dancing through the kitchen wearing nothing but an apron at night. There were ten of us in total and the days were full of group time, but the romance of the place was overwhelming.

As DJ and I strolled the beach one late afternoon, we were caught in a tropical downpour. We ran back to the villa, and I curled up soaking wet in his arms. He whispered in my ear about wedding dates.

"How does May sound?" he mused.

"A year from May?" I asked.

"No, this May."

It was January.

"Let's take our time," I said, leaning my head on his shoulder. It all seemed so fast. Too fast. Although I had always wanted to get married in May. Later I learned he'd already bought the URL—my first name with his last. Which is basically the same thing as a ring when you're dating in the digital age.

This was what I'd always wanted, wasn't it? I was being swept off my feet, wasn't I? This was what every girl wanted.

So why didn't I feel peace?

Looking Perfect

Shortly after our trip to Nicaragua, DJ took me on another international trip, this time to Germany, where he'd been asked to speak at a conference. We landed a few days early, and he stood with me in the departures gate at Frankfurt.

"See all those flights?" He pointed to the old-fashioned departures board.

I nodded.

"Choose any place you see, and we'll go there for the weekend." He grinned. "But the next flight to London leaves in three hours. I know you've never been."

We did go to London, and it was lovely. It was London! But something in me was beginning to disconnect. Slowly, gradually. My heart wasn't feeling heard.

We dated through that year, as I fielded inquiries left and right about when the "date" would be. I was coordinating weddings on weekends to pay the rent in those days, and he ran several well-known businesses in the wedding industry. This was a modern fairytale in the making—or at least the backdrop of a box-office romantic comedy.

But there was no comedy, Ash, because DJ's business took a dive during the financial crisis that year. All his emotional energy and attention turned toward it. We saw each other every day, and he still talked about marriage, but I felt less and less like he knew me. The real me. I felt like I fit into a picture of what he thought his life should look like by thirty, which included being a millionaire and married. That year he turned twenty-nine.

DJ took a tour bus around the country that summer, drawing crowds in every city. His following had never been larger, but he was navigating his own personal crises. I got lost in the midst of it all—a tiny comet circling the rim of a black hole.

Walking alone through a crowd at a trade show in Las Vegas, I was approached by two middle-aged women wearing lanyards.

"Allie!" they screamed. I turned but didn't recognize their faces.

They introduced themselves, exclaiming, "You and DJ are *all* the rage in Arkansas!"

All the rage in Arkansas? DJ had written about us occasionally on his blog, posting pictures and travel stories. Was I going to spend the rest of my life not being known by my partner, while being recognized publicly from his blog posts?

I joined DJ on the tour bus that summer for a few weeks of the speaking tour. One night I looked around at the people on the bus. I saw his driver, his assistant, his photographer, his friend, his videographer, his tour manager, and myself, his girlfriend. I felt like a piece in a puzzle. I would smile at events and take pictures with fans and talk about how wonderful he was, and then I would curl up in my tiny bunk at night and cry myself to sleep. It wasn't until I woke up crying again one morning that I finally admitted something was wrong.

You see, Ash, my relationship with DJ was a lot like our trip to the island. It was a crazy, exhilarating, wondrous, outrageous adventure that looked so perfect and idyllic from the outside. But it was a lot more than you could see in the pictures.

The first three days on Little Eden really had been *that* perfect. But then the biting gnats flared up across the sand, leaving welts all over our legs, and the hot water went out completely as we shivered in cold showers at night. My friend Jasmine was bitten by a bug on her ring finger, and we had to saw off her wedding band as she screamed. That was before the tropical storm hit, sending coconuts flying and tearing at the very beams of the villa. At first it was wild, then kind of scary, then outright violent. We had no connection to the outside world, no way to escape. When the storm let up eventually, we discovered that anything left outside had been lost. The next night the island's generator malfunctioned and burst into flames. We grabbed buckets and wastebaskets and filled them with water from the pool, running, yelling, frantically trying to put out the fire.

The island was a wonderful adventure, and it made for great pictures. But like most journeys, the hard stuff doesn't make it into the photos. I'm a better person because I went for a visit, but I wouldn't want to live there.

That's how some relationships turn out, darling girl.

And you just won't know until you try.

The storm was coming to the island.

The Wrong One

Ash, this relationship of yours is new, and I can't tell you whether it's the right relationship or not. You alone can know that. You are the only one, besides him, who is actually in it.

But you keep asking me if I think he's the wrong guy for you, so what I will tell you is this:

I have found that when you are in the wrong—and I mean, *truly* wrong—relationship, your heart feels like it's drowning. Maybe you're not out of oxygen yet, but you feel wholly submerged, suspended in time and space. Disoriented about what is up and what is down, what is right and what is wrong. The space around you is dark, so dark it's almost impossible to tell you're even underwater. Confusion sets in, and your heart starts to rationalize that water is all that ever existed in the first place. You begin to believe this is normal.

If another friend told you this subaquatic tale, you'd tell her to swim hard for shore—this is not the guy for her. But, you think, *this* guy is different. No one knows him like you do.

That's when delirium kicks in.

You see visions of how great the relationship has been, like flashbacks in Super 8 film. These bright-spot memories are generally caused by the lack of oxygen, and it feels bearable, almost enjoyable. *Maybe this will work*, you muse. The problem is, darling one, you can't stay here. The pressure will pull you down, slowly drowning your joy, suffocating your dreams.

Deciding to end an unhealthy relationship will take every ounce of courage you possess, and more than you knew you had in you. It is making the decision to swim again.

That first moment you decide to paddle up with conviction and clarity will be like catching a glimpse of the light once more. As the rays ripple above like silk, you'll realize the sun never left you. And once you've seen it, you'll scramble toward the light, pulling against the water with every ounce of energy you have, flailing arms and limbs until at last your fingertips touch sky and you burst through the surface and *gasp*. Choking on the sweet taste of air, you'll cough out the water again, and again, and again.

Something changes when you come up for air from a bad relationship. When you've broken the surface and entered the light. You can have the conversation you never believed you had the strength for. You can rise. You can end it. You can be free.

So, my answer to your question, Ash, is simply another question.

Is your relationship underwater, sweet friend? Or is it sailing in the light? Are you swallowing the sea, or are you breathing the life-giving air?

If it's the former, you swim—as hard and as fast as you can. I'm talking Olympian water polo, high-elbow free strokes. If it's the latter, you dance—and take comfort in the sand beneath your toes.

Just remember: your heart cannot dance if it's drowning.

The Breakup

I became so unhappy in the last months of my relationship with DJ. And I should mention, Ash, I think the world of him today. DJ is one of the greatest guys I know, with a heart bigger than the state of Texas. I am honored to call him a friend. But looking perfect on paper and in pictures did not mean we were right for each other, and neither of us was ready for marriage.

There were so many nights when I walked along the Biltmore Wall and cried out to God in confusion and agony. One of DJ's best friends sat me down that last month to share her concerns. "I don't think he supports you, Allie," she said. "You're going to lose yourself to this." But it wasn't until DJ told me he wanted to spend Christmas alone, that he might still have feelings for his ex, and that he wasn't sure he even loved me . . . that I decided the end had come.

Actually, we all decided.

I was twenty-two, sitting on my bed with Christie and my roommates, Brooke and Tricia, talking over our plans to move out of the good ol' Country Club Apartments in a few weeks' time. It was the end of an era. Then out of nowhere I started crying. First one dragging tear, and then another, until a water park opened for business on my face.

The girls looked stunned, then jumped to console me: "The move will be okay! Did we say something wrong?" I finally caught enough breath to process the cause of my tears.

As I listed my heartbreaks, one by one, and how I planned to stay with DJ despite them all, the tears slowly but surely let up. We processed what I'd said in silence. I looked up at my girlfriends then, and it hit me. It hit us all.

"We need to break up."

They talked it over gently, nodding in agreement. We determined that bandages were best ripped off, and tonight was better than someday.

"Shall we go now?" said Brooke.

"Give me a minute." I sniffed. We sat in silence awhile longer, my friends existing in that painful place with me.

Until finally I whispered, "I'm ready." And I was.

I messaged DJ that I was coming over, and the girls drove me up to his house—a place he used to call "our house" because he said it was where we would build a home someday. The girls waited in the car. "Thirty minutes, and we're coming in for you." Knowing they were near imbued me with a strength I didn't know I could possess.

DJ must have seen this coming, but he cried as I told him, nonetheless.

I didn't cry. I had already hit the bottom of sorrow's well. I had no more tears left to give.

The girls took me out for sushi afterward, and I ate in a daze. It was a new restaurant that hadn't sorted out its kitchen yet, and when we got home our clothes reeked of raw fish and eel sauce. Jackets, shirts, and bras alike. We hung everything outside that night, like the memories. I knew I could carry them with me someday, but not until they'd aired out a bit.

"Choose your girlfriends wisely," the old saying goes. "They will probably outlive your husband."

Ending Well

When it comes to endings, Ash, begin by remembering who you are.

Our hearts can get so wound up in another's that we forget to see ourselves as a wholly separate person. You have your own story, dear girl, *apart* from this guy. Your lives have intersected, yes, but the experience of this relationship is only a snapshot of who you are and what you will do in your future days.

You must trust your gut, and you mustn't play out the what-ifs. Don't imagine your wedding, or your children, or the next fifteen years of Christmases and cookouts and soccer games. Or in this case, vacations under Siena sunsets. Do not do that. If this is not the boy for you, there is no sense fabricating memories that will never exist, or practicing your signature with his last name. Stay in the now, in what you know to be true.

And remember: if he makes you feel not good enough, he is not good enough for you.

Regardless of what happens, I love you. I am for you. And I am proud of you, with or without this fella.

In your boat,

x

He loved me in extremes
In scorching sun and numbing cold
There was no in between
And I the lonely traveler
Who could not dress the part
Found parkas on the summer of my heart
And left for temperate days
Of clouds and light.

UNKNOWN

CHAPTER 15

ON PERFECTION & FAILING

Perfect means shallow and unreal
and fatally uninteresting.

ANNE LAMOTT

JANUARY 12

Ash,

I know we've talked this through backward and forward, but I'll say it once more that I'm proud of you. Leaving the wrong relationship is about the bravest thing a girl can do.

I'm also so happy you're home from your semester abroad! And in the same time zone, at last.

Cherish the memories and the journeys you had, darling girl; treasure them up in your heart. Store up the lessons you learned from the mistakes you made, the thrills from the risks you took, the growth you gained from going so far outside your comfort zone the GPS no longer registered a location.

I know your mind is reeling now that you're home. The end of a relationship, the transition back to the States . . . and the fact that friends with whom you once shared everything will never understand what you've experienced. Take time to sit with these things, Ash. Spend a moment with all of them. Let the waves of memory hit your rocky soul and soak it, then explore the wonder of living things left behind in the tide pools of your heart. Talk to God as you stroll that spiritual shore. The living things left behind are yours alone to behold.

Missed Connections

When traveling we find new vistas, and that's why most people journey. But the greatest adventures, the kind that shape our inner beings, happen when we experience more than new landscapes. They happen when we find ourselves in need.

We are so in control of our day-to-day lives, Ash, that we lose the sense of mystery found when we journey to an unfamiliar place. When things fall outside our control. When we fail.

Before I moved away from Santa Barbara, I took a trip for work that went nothing like I'd planned. Have you had some trips like that? I'd been asked to go to Alabama to meet with a family foundation interested in giving us a grant for an anti-slavery project in Southeast Asia. I was nervous and thrilled, envisioning the impact their funding could make.

As I pulled away from home that Friday evening, I realized I'd left my ticket sitting in the printer and almost turned back. *No matter*, I thought, *easy enough to print at the airport*.

Except it wasn't.

I hit traffic on my way to LAX, which was more packed than a sold-out night at Madison Square Garden. Turns out it was spring break. My heart sank as I ran inside. A warning sign on the kiosk alerted me I'd missed the cutoff for ticket printing. By one minute.

"No . . ." I exclaimed. "No, no, no!"

I sprinted to the check-in desk, where they sent me to the

help desk, where I politely begged the line of grumpy travelers to let me cut in front. Breathless, I faced the man at the counter.

"I *could* print your ticket," he mused, "but you're going to miss it anyway."

"Please!" I begged. "Just let me try."

The TSA, always so attentive when you're rushed, decided to search my bag that night, piece by piece. And then I sprinted, sweaty and shaking, to a closed departure door. My stomach dropped like a discarded dress.

"We just closed it," said the agent flatly. She pointed me back out, past security, to the rebooking desk.

Everything was sold out to Atlanta that night, the closest major airport to Alabama, so they put me on standby.

As each flight's departure drew near, I wiggled my way toward the front, sitting by my suitcase on the carpet where I could see the standby list on the monitor. I watched my name inch closer and closer to the top, and then the door would close. My stomach would roll to the floor once more. Eventually the buzzing departures hall faded into a ghost town of empty chairs and candy wrappers, and it was just me and the vacuum guy circling the carpet. I remade my PowerPoint presentation in the corner at three a.m. It was the only productive thing I could do.

At five a.m. McDonald's opened, and I lined up like a worker receiving rations in the Great Depression. The airport flooded with fresh faces, and I sat on the floor with my Egg McMuffin and black coffee and read the Gospels and prayed. I hate going to God when I'm desperate like that.

When I didn't make it on the nine a.m. flight, I called my mom and broke down sobbing. I'd missed my presentation slot completely. On the fifth standby, I was allowed onto the plane, and I boarded like it was a lifeboat departing the *Titanic*. I emailed the foundation in defeat, determined to make the journey, missed presentation or not.

We're picking you up! said the message from my mom. My parents were, incidentally, visiting my cousins in Atlanta, and—given that I hadn't slept all night—didn't want me driving to Alabama on my own. As the plane's wheels touched down in Georgia, another message popped up on my phone.

Where are you? What's happening? I'm praying for you.

It was from Sue, whom I've taken to calling my prayer mentor. Sue is one of those people who just seems a little closer to the heavens than the rest of us. She listens when God speaks, and dreams dreams that mean things—the way I've always wished I could. I usually dream that I'm falling or have forgotten to wear pants. Sue has mentored countless young women at our church. She's the sort of woman you want praying for you.

"Pay attention," Sue would tell me. "God is working all around us, but you must pay attention to see it."

Call it what you will, but something moved in Sue's spirit to pray for me that day. I guess she was paying attention. The message alone made me cry. Even if all of the funding was lost, I knew I wasn't forgotten in my failure.

Salutatorian

Let's talk about failure for a moment, Ash. I got your message that you didn't get the part-time job. Or the scholarship. That's a lot of tough news in two weeks.

It's okay to feel like a failure, dear girl. I feel like a failure at least twice a week—and frequently on Mondays. There are so many dreams I've never pursued. Competitions I've lost, emails I've left unanswered. More people than I can count whom I've let down.

Failure is part of the human condition. We are not only fallible, we're fail-able. We are not only capable of failing, we're prone to it. In the same way we are prone to overeating when good food is on the table. If we are willing to try, we must be willing to fail.

Again, and again, and again.

Do you know how badly I wanted to make valedictorian in high school, Ash? Straight As was *who I was*! Until I was late one too many times for—ironically—leadership class at 7:15 a.m. and I received a B plus. Ridiculous, I know. But a tiny part of me was crushed to be the salutatorian at graduation that next spring. It felt like a shamed salute to imperfection, until I realized my crusty, perfectionist ego probably needed a demotion. I was forced to accept the fact that I was more than the grades I made. Or didn't make.

Sometimes failure can save us from ourselves.

Failure teaches us we can miss the mark and still be okay. We can fail and still wake up the next morning and be our same selves—albeit a little more humble.

I know I'll fail in life, just like I know I'll get colds, on occasion. I accept it as a fact, so I'm not devastated when it happens. I'm human. At the same time, I don't live in daily fear of it. When I get sick with the common cold, I try to focus on having the best sick day ever. With cozy blankets and rom-coms and as much hot tea as my mug can hold.

In the same way, when we fail, why not have the best failure ever? Why not simmer in it and try to let its lessons sink in? Failure is an opportunity to not take ourselves too seriously.

The Slopes

Sometimes we fail because we've fumbled. Other times we fail because we dared to try.

My mom was raised in upstate New York, where skiing was

a popular pastime. She spent most of her childhood weekends on the slopes, so she was as comfortable on her skis as she was on her feet. I'll never forget one of our family ski trips, as I awkwardly made my way down the bunny hill, she explained to me that if she didn't fall at least once each day she would be disappointed.

"You mean you actually *want* to fall?" I said, feet up and frustrated as I wiggled my rear end out of a snowdrift. "But why would you want to fall?"

"Because, honey," she laughed, "if I don't fall, then I know I'm not challenging myself to improve—I'm just playing it safe. If I don't fall, it means I'm not pushing myself to become a better skier."

I never shared my mom's problem of fall-free skiing during a day on the slopes. Actually, it was rare when I hadn't fallen fourteen times by the end of a run. But her advice became a gem of wisdom for me.

I'm not immune to failure, Ash. No one is, and I don't think we should want to be. An immunity to failure would mean we never ventured beyond our zone of comfort, and I don't want a life where I'm not brave enough to try.

Sometimes enduring the biggest failures gives us the freedom to risk greater feats in the future. It is only in overcoming the fear of failure that we can ever take the risks we need to follow our calling. Maturing isn't about failing less. It's about failing better. It's planning for success while never being surprised by failure when it comes. Maturity means standing at the door when failure comes knocking and saying, "Ah, I thought you might drop by," instead of cowering somewhere in a corner.

Look to any great leader or legend, and you'll likely find multidimensional failure. Abraham Lincoln had a nervous breakdown and lost multiple congressional and senatorial runs before he became president. Dr. Seuss was rejected by twenty-seven publishers before his first book went to print.[1] This is why I love reading biographies and Wikipedia pages when they tell the whole story. Oftentimes we only see the polished end products of people's lives, and it's important to remember that sometimes the most successful people also made the most mistakes.

Failure is the signal that we're trying beyond our comfort zone, beyond our ability to be perfect. The older I get, the more I'm convinced that successful people aren't people who don't fail. Successful people are those who have learned to fail, successfully.

Alabama

I'll never forget seeing my parents' red rental car pulling up to Hartsfield-Jackson the afternoon after my flight failure marathon. I fell into their hugs as they threw my suitcase in the trunk.

Ash, I used to think my parents only wanted to be with me to celebrate successes—and of course they do—but I realized somewhere in early adulthood that they also want to be there for the failures and sorrows. They don't just want the goal posts; they want to be with me on the journey. The highs and the lows—the whole thing. Yours do too.

The head of the foundation emailed me back, expressing concern for my travel woes. She said the granddaughter who had put us forward originally had presented to the finance council in my stead. Then she invited me to dinner with their entire extended family. We pulled into Alabama hours later with time to spare, and I changed into my navy-blue dress in a Starbucks bathroom, applying mascara with a grin in the dim yellow light.

I fell in love with the forty-plus people at their family dinner that evening. I moved around the room meeting aunts and uncles and cousins and grandparents. Before dessert, they asked me to stand up and share about our work, and I did so to an enthusiastic response.

Suffice it to say, they funded our project. And I learned we are not a lost cause in our failures. In our missed connections and misconceptions and mistakes, there can come a greater good. Sometimes in spite of our failures, and other times because of them.

Failure reminds us how much we need one another in prayer and work and partnership. We cannot do it all, and we certainly cannot do it well alone.

Beauty of Imperfection

If failure is an integral part of the human story, then why do we war against it so much? For me, it comes down to a core desire to not only have success, but to have perfection. The tyranny of the need to be perfect is a struggle I've had for as long as I've been able to say the word *perfect*. But there is beauty in imperfection, Ash.

During those childhood years, my parents saved for one big vacation every summer to visit our extended family in the Southeast. Each year we would eat fresh blueberries and fried chicken at family reunions and explore the Biltmore Estate in Asheville and hold our breath through the mountain tunnels of the Blue Ridge Parkway and sift for gems at "mining" outposts. Every year I would beg to stay there longer, certain I was about to find a ruby. Still yet to happen.

Summers for Adam and me were all sticky heat and fireflies and thunderstorms. One of our many traditions was attending the local folk art shows, which is something you can count on when you grow up with a mom who's an art teacher. We would yawn and stare lazily at the giant quilts that claimed the walls of folk art museums and craft festivals. Then one year, my brother and I looked closely at one of the museum-quality quilts.

"Mom!" we exclaimed. "There's a piece upside down!" This was almost as exciting as finding a ruby at the rock-sifting quarry.

It turns out, as my mom explained, many of the great quilters in the South insert a piece upside down before they finish. Or an incorrect stitch, or a mismatched scrap of patchwork. This is the "only God is perfect" mark. A reminder to every onlooker that we are not perfect, nor is our work.

All of nature is imperfect, and yet we do not judge it as such. We don't look at the daisies in a field or the birds in the air or the waves on the shore and compare them to a picture we have of how we think they should be. The imperfection of nature is the very diversity that makes it wild and wonderful and real. If we, too, are natural beings, why then do we judge ourselves with an expectation of perfection?

The drive for perfection often comes down to fear. Fear of not controlling the results, of not making enough of an impact, of not doing or saying the right thing. When we reclaim the beauty of imperfection, like the quilters, we release perfection's mighty control over our lives. We can find joy in our imperfections.

Consider the time I sent a mass email with a typo at our nonprofit—every communication person's worst nightmare. "It's all right." Our president, Dave, shrugged. "It makes us lovable."

The Willows

We expect ourselves to be perfect, as well as our experiences. Experiences can disappoint us just as much, but it doesn't mean we can't let them teach us.

I love that you went to volunteer at the Willows, sweet

friend. What an opportunity to meet, spend time with, and serve this assisted-living community alongside your fellow students.

I know you didn't love (okay, hated) your afternoon there, but Ash, I want to encourage you to go back. Ask yourself why you disliked it so much—what fear or discomfort did it stir in you? Then lean into that. You might have something to learn here. This community might have something to teach you, and you, in turn, might have something beautiful to offer them.

As my Grandma Emma would say, "It's okay if you don't like doin' it. Just start doin'. The feelings will follow."

Think about it, will you?

Going back might be the perfect thing for you to do.

Lovingly,

x

It is not the critic who counts; not the man who points out how the strong man stumbles or where the doer of deeds could have done them better. The credit belongs to the man who is actually in the arena, whose face is marred by dust and sweat and blood; who strives valiantly; who errs, who comes short again and again, because there is no effort without error and shortcoming; but who does actually strive to do the deeds; who knows great enthusiasms, the great devotions; who spends himself in a worthy cause; who at the best knows in the end the triumph of high achievement, and who at the worst, if he fails, at least fails while daring greatly, so that his place shall never be with those cold and timid souls who neither know victory nor defeat.

THEODORE ROOSEVELT

CHAPTER 16

ON DREAMS & CALLING

The journey is the destination.

DAN ELDON

MARCH 13

Dear Ash,

I'm proud of you for going back to the Willows. I know it made you uncomfortable, but it's a place that might need you—and you just might need it as well.

I love that you've made friends there already. Donny sounds hilarious, and Martha, what a joy! I can't believe the stories Archie has been telling. That one's a flirtatious old fellow. How many times did you say you've been this week? And you're bringing other students with you? The residents must love that.

I think throwing them a senior prom is a fabulous idea. Count me in, of course. I'll bring my dancing shoes.

Impact

Speaking of generations, did you know we're being called the "me" generation, Ash? Yes—that's me and you. I've heard us called selfish, selfie-oriented, self-obsessed. Entitled, entertainment-crazed, experience-needy. Maybe we are, but I think we're something awfully special too. Our generation has been hard-wired in a historically unique way. We've grown up speaking technology, watched wars unfold before our eyes, and witnessed a bulletproof economy collapse. We're open-eyed, battle-tried, seaworthy. We want more than a picket fence and a pocketbook. We crave authenticity, impact, legacy.

Ash, we are in a unique moment in history. Did you know that the majority of young people entering the job market today care more about purpose than profit? Our generation cares more about making a difference than making money. I love that.

There is a myth floating around lately, though, that only social enterprises and nonprofits create impact. This just isn't true. Business, all business, creates impact. Period. Whether it's saving the lives of children and preserving the environment, or exploiting children for labor and polluting the oceans.

I get so excited when young people want to start nonprofits and social enterprises. *I love it.* That wasn't the fad so much when I was graduating. But I also don't want to see us perpetuate the dichotomy of two separate and mutually exclusive directions for work, because this dichotomy is part of the very problem at the core of our broken systems.

I've heard the earliest Puritans who came to America were actually capitalists by nature. Being very devout, they felt guilty for the business acumen driving them, and in accordance with their spiritual beliefs, they had to do penance for their financial gain. Hence, the creation of distinct for-profit and not-for-profit entities.[1]

It wasn't long before this model evolved into a take-with-your-left, give-with-your-right mentality that has permeated our capitalistic culture ever since. You're either taking or you're giving. And that thinking alone has allowed companies to do irreparable damage to the world while being celebrated for cutting ribbons and taking tax write-offs.

Change the World

I look at the company my dad and his brothers own and run, which has been in our family since the 1950s. It has provided hundreds of jobs through the years and served countless people across the community with products as simple as art and office supplies. Their work has been as noble as quietly donating resources for children's art therapy and as practical as stocking the right shade of cerulean blue so an artist can capture the sky.

It's a company that benefits our community.

Then I look at certain nonprofits that seem to take so much money and deliver so little in the way of impact. Not all, by any means. Ash, you know how passionate I am about nonprofits. But some of them make less positive impact than they'd like people to think. Maybe the communities they serve actually just need jobs so they can create their own stable futures. Maybe the heads of those NGOs just need a pat on the back and an ego check.

Working in a nonprofit or a mission-based company will not necessarily fulfill the need for purpose in your life. I've known too many wonderful people in fabulous organizations who felt devoid of meaning. We each need to find our purpose for ourselves, both through and apart from our work. Meaningful work, no matter how good, will not alone give our lives meaning.

Calling is comprehensive; it spans the whole of who we are. From our vocation to our character to our relationships, and everything in between.

I no longer believe we need to go "change the world," Ash, because the world is always changing. I'd rather think of myself as improving the world, because the world is not always improving. Plus, changing the world feels insurmountable most days. It's a task too big for anyone, and I fear we'll be paralyzed by the overwhelming thought of working toward it. Improvement, however, can be measured in the smallest of increments.

This is why we should never couch our identity in the difference we're making around the globe, because we are all called to different impact in different places. The guy who beats the drum in the band is not meant to sound like the fellow playing the tuba. They both bring something different to the music.

For some people, impact will look like my brother responding to humanitarian crises in Haiti and South Sudan and serving displaced people. For others, impact means delivering the mail, fulfilling an order, or keeping the system online, while building into their family, friends, and community at large.

In the end, isn't that our aim? Healthy, thriving communities that support and take care of one another, everywhere. Remember, we have doctors because people get sick, but cities wouldn't run if we all became doctors. Or NGO leaders.

Girl Bosses

Young women today don't believe in themselves nearly as much as young men do, Ash.[2]

These stats are strange, because there are actually more women in college today than men. We are *plenty* smart. Just look at the boys around you! No offense to your male friends.

Someone once told me that, when it comes to our dreams, we can't imagine it if we can't see it modeled. Maybe we're not lacking in raw talent, but rather, in representation?

I have a friend named Vera who is one of the best girl bosses I know. She started a company out of her bedroom that impacts countless lives, grosses millions annually, and has never taken a penny from investors. She is interviewed and photographed left and right and looks like the coolest, most successful girl on the proverbial block.

But she feels like a failure. She feels like a failure because her family wanted her to be an A-list actress and she is not.

Worse than that, she feels unattractive. This gets my blood boiling. She thinks being a CEO, running a company, managing people, making big decisions, and impacting lives does not fit the cultural norm of what's attractive. I should add, she's drop-dead gorgeous, but that seems to have no bearing on the light in which she views herself. She does not fit into the cultural mold. To look pretty, to perform, to say nothing.

I wonder what Vera's inner life would be like if she'd had role models who were running companies and organizations and schools, and not just looking sexy for men's magazines.

When she told me she thought businesswomen were unattractive, it made me so mad I wanted to start a business.

Spiritual MASH

I didn't learn the true importance of role models until high school—a time of discovery and wonder and growth for me and my girlfriends. Was yours the same?

One evening our summer youth group leader, Morgan, sat my small group down to teach us about the concept of spiritual gifts and help us discern ours. I'm the type of girl who loves all types of personality tests and quizzes because I like it when a piece of paper tells me things I didn't know about myself. That is to say, I was excited.

We sat in my friend's basement in wide-eyed wonder, anxious to see what holy mysteries this exercise would reveal. Morgan gave us each a piece of paper and a chewed-up ballpoint pen.

"I want you to list five people you admire in the world," she instructed. "People you look up to for how they love God and love others—people you want to be like."

Heads went down. This was practically seminary school! We took a few thoughtful minutes to craft our lists and put down our pens before Morgan continued.

"Now I want you to list the attribute you admire most in each of them."

Heads went down again, this time brows furrowed. I listed my Auntie Fawn, for her wisdom. My mom, for her servant's heart.

We waited for the big reveal. Perhaps we would rearrange the letters in their names to reveal a divine calling. Maybe we'd order them into a crisscross chart like the game MASH to predict our future. You remember, don't you? "Mansion, Apartment, Shack, House"—the most popular slumber party game. There were so many boys I was convinced I would marry and live in a mansion with . . . Actually, I hope you didn't play that game.

"All of the attributes you listed in the people you admire most—those are your gifts," Morgan said. "Those are the things God is seeking to develop in your lives. That's why you're drawn to them in the people you admire."

We put down our pens and stared at our lists before sharing them eagerly with one another. The results were even more exciting than MASH.

Role Models

We need to know who we admire, Ash, and why. Otherwise we default to thinking that the girls in the mascara ads are the only measure of who we ought to be.

Seek out women who inspire you. Women who capture some

spark of your aspiring self, women leading the kind of life you dream of living. The type of women Vera didn't have to look up to. Even if you end up in an entirely different vocation, the very act of dreaming will guide you toward who you're meant to be. The glimmer of what you admire in them may help you discover something completely unique about yourself.

This is why I believe so firmly in mentorship, and also in championing other people—specifically, other women—who are living in ways that can and should be a model for the rest of us. Those who show us good or impossible things can be done because they are doing them.

On the Shoulders

When my brother was in high school, he bought a book of photojournalism work by a reporter named Dan Eldon—the youngest Reuters reporter in history.[3] Have you heard of him, Ash? In the nineties Dan bravely documented the atrocities of the conflict in Somalia and was tragically killed in the midst of it. Dan's journey sparked a light inside my little brother that pointed him toward the aid work he does to this day. Dan's photos and notes and way of living, always on display atop our family's coffee table, inspired me too. Dan made me want to live a bigger story.

And my brother and I weren't the only ones.

Dan's life led my friend Jason and his buddies to take a trip to Uganda in the early 2000s, where they stumbled upon a group of child soldiers who'd been brutalized by a warlord named Joseph Kony. From there they launched an organization called Invisible Children, which would later lead to the most viral video of all time, but not before their first scrappy documentary made its round of screenings at Westmont the fall of my sophomore year.

My brother and my friend, Linda, showing me the beauty of Haiti.

Were they young and unqualified and imperfect? Of course. And because of that, they showed me and my peers that we were not too young or unqualified or imperfect to make an inch of difference in this broken, brutal world. We had been given much, and we were not too young to do *something* about the atrocities that raged on our planet.

When I began working in the anti-slavery movement, I knew human trafficking was a major global issue, with more slaves in the world today than at any point in history. What I didn't know was that I'd stepped into a much greater story. This was the fourth abolition movement in modern history— preceded by the Belgian abolition movement to free Congolese slaves in the mid-1900s, preceded by the American movement led by Lincoln and abolitionists in the mid-1800s, preceded by the English abolition movement led by Wilberforce in the early 1800s.

Each of us, Ash, is born into a specific time and place in history, with certain abilities and opportunities to make an impact on our global needs. No one is making this up from scratch. We each are a single thread knit into the fabric of some greater tapestry. All we see, from our perspective, are the messy strings on the back side. We see knots and loose ends and an imperfect process that can and should be critiqued. But together we are building a masterpiece.

Leaders, social movements, and legislative actions have paved the roads before us. We have communal stories and collective impact. We stand on the shoulders of giants, as the saying goes. And because of that, we are not meant to journey these courses alone.

Our culture, high on individualism, tells us we ought to, Ash. It tells us our careers and our callings are a one-man or one-woman show. But this is wrong, and painfully so. Dr. King once said, "We are tied together in the single garment of destiny."[4] My pastor in San Francisco, Dave, wrote about this in another way. We tend to know our truest selves as individuals, but what, he asks, if our identity actually exists in relation to others? In relation to God, to our family, to our friends, to our world?[5] Even God, in Christian theology, exists as a trinity: Father, Son, and Holy Spirit.

God is a relationship.

Study any revolutionary, and you'll find that those who took on something greater than themselves, great enough to change the course of history, never saw the fullness of their dream to completion. My friend Justin reminded me of this the other day. Abraham Lincoln never saw the end of slavery, Martin Luther King Jr. never saw the Civil Rights Act signed, and Moses never touched the promised land. The most worthy struggles, for justice and equality and peace, continue to this day. The leaders we reflect on with such respect and admiration were signposts in these movements, catalysts who propelled forward a vaster, historic good.

There is an old Chinese proverb that says, "Each generation will reap what the former generation has sown." We benefit from and carry forward the dreams of those who've come before us and cleared the way. And we, in turn, will lay a foundation for the generations coming after us. They will carry on the dreams we envision but never complete. And in this way we run a communal relay race with those of the past and those of the future, as we carry and pass on the torch of our day.

Dreams

Do you have a vision for your future, Ash? Mine used to be quite clear. At around five years old, I asked my mom what the most important job in the world was. "Well," she mused, "president, I suppose." (Now she wishes she'd said *mother.*) From then onward, I wanted to be president.

One of the first people I told was my hairstylist. She had short dark hair and worked at a Supercuts in the strip mall by my favorite frozen yogurt shop. As I sat in her chair, feet high above the floor, she asked me in a somewhat condescending voice what I wanted to be when I grew up. She looked like a cultural savant, so I responded with quiet confidence, "President of the United States." She laughed, as did the young woman working next to her. "How cute!" they exclaimed.

I sank deeper into the red pleather chair, defeated. *One day,* I thought, *she'll look back and be amazed she cut the president's hair.* I imagined sauntering into Supercuts, secret service in tow, and how horrified she'd be at having not gotten an autograph when she had the chance.

My confidence stayed buoyed until one summer a few years later in Asheville, when I explained my reasoned ambition to my grandfather at the dinner table. He shot that dream down so hard it sputtered in toxic fumes on the floor. This time I was crushed. I ran into the guest room, locked the door, curled up in a ball on the hide-a-bed, and cried. I felt silly for taking the criticism so harshly and being unable to control my emotions.

What was I going to do in the face of a national disaster once in office? Yet I could not shake the sting of shattered dreams.

The sad thing is, I was not the first in the family to have my dreams crushed. My grandpa was very old-fashioned, you could say. He believed he knew what was best for my mom in every situation and her input was of no importance. If he could have arranged her marriage, he would have. He also wasn't optimistic about my mom's opportunities in the world as a woman. He was especially not keen on her passion for art.

"You should be a secretary," he would tell her. Which is a fine career, except he believed it was the only thing she could aspire to be. No other option—end of discussion. During typing class in school, my mom would intentionally drop her paper on the floor during tests, trying to prove with her C-minus grades that she would, in fact, make a terrible secretary.

Ash, never let someone sway you from the beauty and the mystery of your dreams. Whether they're superb or superfluous, those tiny dreams taking shelter in your heart will whisper truths to you about your life. It matters less that you achieve them, and more that you know where they're pointing you. That you listen to them long enough to find your path.

We can also change our dreams, Ash. They aren't static but grow with us. We can hold them like a cherished heirloom or toss them out like a cheap souvenir, but no one should throw them out for us.

Called To

Upon leaving my job this past summer, a river of requests came flooding in. They were all good things for me to be involved with, but I struggled to know where to say yes. I needed some bearings, so I outlined my calling. I made a list of five areas I feel drawn to, by which I can judge where and how to spend my time. It may be helpful for you to do the same! Then, as opportunities come along, you can use it as a matrix to decide what's worth committing to.

There are many things I love, but these are the things I feel—and have always felt—*called* to:

1. My tribe. Specifically my family, friends, colaborers, and neighbors. My community. Those whom I've built into, and who consistently build into me.
2. Social justice. Specifically slavery, sitting at the intersection of so many injustices. The poor, the abandoned, the vulnerable; the forgotten, the exploited, the oppressed. Creating a world that's better for them tomorrow than it is today.
3. The church. Wrought with brokenness, beauty, confusion, and hope, as it grows in its understanding—both spiritual and sociopolitical—of what it means to follow Jesus in this culture and moment in history.
4. Young women. A generation with more opportunities than ever, but also more pressure to be, do, and have it all. To speak truth into their lives in a profound and meaningful way and spur them toward their best for this world.
5. The arts. Specifically media—words written and spoken, film, technology, and art. To share ideas and values with others in ways that are creative and inspired, and elevate the common good.

There are many expressions of these callings in my life, and the ways I've pursued them have changed and grown as I have over the years. But I try not to say yes to things now unless they fall in at least three of these buckets.

At Not For Sale, our president, Dave, taught us about the concept of *keiretsu*. It's a Japanese term that refers to the way multiple companies under one greater holding company can all support one another and intersect. We tried to build our non-profit projects, and later our impact investment projects, this way. I've also realized we can form keiretsu across our calling, pursuing things that enhance one another. In fact, everything is benefited when we do.

Some days I resist my calling. Some days I just want to run away and open a lavender shop in a tiny French village. I have fought against my calling and argued with God about why I am here. But ultimately, this is where he's led me, and I would not be *truly* myself if I did not set my bearings in this direction. Life is too short not to do the things I know I'm here to do. I'm learning that being faithful to my calling means saying yes to what is missional, and no to just about everything else.

Still working on it though. Hold me accountable, please?

Sisterhood

We are so privileged, Ash, to be able to pursue our dreams. I believe there is no greater honor than to do work that benefits the soul of another, and that is a mission to which we're all called.

Speaking of: Let's talk about the calling of sisterhood. This conversation you had with Emma sounds like a breakthrough, dear girl. What a gift! What a complete and beautiful gift. I read a quote the other day that said, "Be who you needed when you were younger." I believe you have the opportunity to do that for your sister. Even though she drives you mad at moments (as siblings do), I can't underscore how much she looks up to you, all the same.

Everything you say will carry meaning for her, even when you think she's not listening. Every action is a signal, the way you live a model. The way you cared for her last weekend at home, when you weren't feeling well yourself, shows her what it means to be a servant. To care about another's well-being even more than your own.

I'm so glad she has you in her life.

I'm glad I have you in my life too.

Love you, dear friend,

X

PS—My grandpa may have shot down the prospect of president, but he did always say I should be a writer.

> They who dream by day are cognizant of many things
> which escape those who dream only by night.
>
> *EDGAR ALLEN POE*

CHAPTER 17

ON WORK & WEDDINGS

It had long since come to my attention that people of
accomplishment rarely sat back and let things happen
to them. They went out and happened to things.

LEONARDO DA VINCI

MAY 12

Dear Ash,

This month you're turning twenty-one! And what an incredible young woman you are.

Milestone birthdays are my favorites. Sixteen when you
can drive, eighteen when you can vote, twenty when you're no
longer a teen, and twenty-one when you can enter any estab-
lishment you choose.

And then there's my favorite birthday: twenty-two. The
year we launch into the world. The year the safe ground of student life drops out from underneath our feet and we catapult
forward, awkwardly flying or free-falling (or if you're me, some
combination of the two), surrounded by the air of adulthood.
Baby birds out from the nest. At last we turn from our years
of learning and absorbing, and we begin to contribute in more

grown-up ways. The world expects something of us, and we, in turn, can rise to the occasion.

But you're not twenty-two, yet. So for all of that launching, you will just have to wait!

Let's Talk Work

It's the spring of your junior year, a time that every collegiate student meets with determination, dreams, and duty: time to choose a summer job. Not a career, but a job. And maybe one that's not stationed behind slices of sourdough bread or an ice cream scoop.

Being a junior was an odd and exciting time for me too. I had just returned from Brussels feeling six months older and six thousand miles wiser. I felt like I'd hit my stride and I knew what I was capable of. I wanted a challenge and I wanted to lead.

So when a new opportunity came up that conveniently fell into both those categories, I jumped at the chance: running for class president. I was certain I was the girl for the job, which was so important that you even got a small stipend. But I never found a good campaign slogan, and that's probably where my issues began. "Let's rally, vote for Allie" felt forced.

It pains me to tell you, dear dreamer, that I lost the campaign. And I was devastated. I pretended not to be—at all—but I was. Wasn't this my calling? Wasn't I made to lead twelve hundred college students and represent all that was right and attainable in the world? I was meant to be the liaison to the faculty and the board and the school president. *Me.* Not the supersmart, affable, pre-med guy who actually, completely deservingly, won the election.

Since I didn't end up leading my college into its prime years, creating reforms that would last for decades to come and inspiring the school to commission a statue of me for the rose garden on Kerrwood Lawn, I decided I should get a job.

I was sticking around Santa Barbara that summer, my first summer away from home, and I genuinely needed to pay the rent. An astronomically high four hundred dollars a month for a shared bedroom in the slightly unglamorous and inaptly named, you guessed it, Country Club Apartments.

I was sitting in my dorm room thinking about the summer when it occurred to me this could be the last opportunity to choose a job entirely unrelated to my career. It wasn't, but I felt like it might be at the time. So I sat on my bed and rolled the thought around: *If I could do anything, what would I do?*

Scuba instructor was out because I didn't know how to scuba dive yet. Actress was also out, for obvious reasons. And so I came down to one vivid and alluring dream: a wedding planner. Visions of J.Lo flashed through my mind. The sleek cream dress, the headset, the perfectly coiffed bun speeding past a sea of pink peonies to meet the frazzled bride and calm her nervous fears before sending her gracefully down the aisle toward the man of her dreams.

I loved the idea of the high-society world that surrounded extravagant weddings. These elegant affairs would be a world away from the hippy-surfer beach town where I grew up, and I thought it seemed like an excellent way to attend glamorous events and taste wedding cake and maybe even meet a handsome groomsman. Just being honest.

Oh, and I also loved "love," and the dream of marriage, and the lifelong commitments, and the emotional stream of tears, and being involved in *the most important day* of someone's life. There was also that.

Envisioning the endless frosting flavors I would try and how sophisticated my hair would look in a topknot, I Googled "wedding planners in Santa Barbara." I found three, emailed them, and sat back to wait.

The first two were silent, like good wedding guests when the minister asks for objections. But the third responded immediately. *Jackie Blackwell.* Even her name sounded elegant. She was looking for an assistant and wanted to meet me at the Biltmore Hotel for a glass of wine. I was newly twenty-one and had never had a business meeting over wine. If this was what the working world felt like, then punch my time card and call me an employee.

Two hours later, after a power handshake on my ten-dollars-an-hour wage and a glass of chardonnay as golden as the rings I would hand the best man, we had an agreement. I would be an assistant wedding planner. *Opah!*

The Generator

Do you remember how I told you to begin by saying yes and diving in? That's what I did in my wedding-planning days.

I had only coordinated one wedding as an assistant when another wedding-planner called my boss and asked if she might be available to assist on an upcoming high-profile event. Jackie was busy but gave the woman my info. We talked, and she offered to pay me a whopping thirty bucks an hour to assist. I could hardly believe it!

This Montecito wedding was the epitome of high-society glamour I'd dreamed about. Mounds of blush roses amid winding garden pathways, guests dressed in flowing gowns and tuxedos who laughed and sipped dry champagne. A photographer approached and introduced herself, explaining she was covering the event for *British Vogue*. British Vogue! I'd never picked up a copy, but it sure sounded fancy. I couldn't remember ever attending an event so stylish. Coming from Santa Cruz, I thought Roxy surf clothing was couture until I got to college.

I quickly learned that the coordinator was a friend of the bride's family. I also learned that, because she was a friend, she wanted to enjoy the wedding just like all the other guests. So, when the dinner reception came, she took a seat and handed me the clipboard. I've heard it said that a diamond is just a piece of coal that did well under pressure, and this stone was about to be polished.

That was the day I learned how to run between gravel and grass in high heels. You take long strides on the balls of your feet, heels in the air, like a bear lumbering about in ballerina slippers. Back and forth I ran between the catering station and the band and the dining tables and the bride, making decisions on the fly. The coordinator laughed with guests and drank champagne and reveled in the success of her setup, but the caterer took notice of the scene.

"How many weddings have you done?" she asked. One, I explained. But it was a very nice one.

The next morning I got a slew of emails from the perceptive caterer connecting me to other coordinators in Santa Barbara and LA, explaining that if they needed an assistant, I was their girl. From there my employment prospects widened. I worked often with another wedding planner, Alexandra, who planned *really* big, four-coordinator affairs and allowed me to run around with a headset on. J.Lo vision, achieved!

Later that summer, I found myself coordinating a wedding at that same ethereal estate where it'd all begun. I was darting to and fro trying to corral the extended family for photos, which is not unlike herding cats, when the lighting technician approached sheepishly and asked if I might come look at the generator.

"Is it urgent?" I pressed.

"Um, well, I mean," he stammered, "it's . . . yeah, I think it's urgent."

I followed him behind the tent, where I discovered our single generator, the size of a small baby elephant, rocking rapidly from side to side and spewing billows of smoke.

"Yes," I said to the technician, "this would be urgent."

It took thirty minutes to get another generator delivered, which felt like three hours. Then the technician informed us it would take another three minutes to get the new generator switched over, which meant that for the length of a radio pop single, the entire reception tent and ten-person band and thirty-person catering crew would not have power. *Oy vey.*

I ran to the catering area, called out, "Hold the food!" then dashed to the band and whispered to the lead singer as he played. When they finished the song, I hissed into the headset, "Cut power—*now!*" The chandeliers dimmed, and the band went silent. Thankfully it was only dusk, and the waning summer daylight refracted its glow into the darkened tent.

"Bride has not noticed," I whispered. "Repeat, bride has not noticed." There are very few things-gone-wrong that are worth mentioning to a bride on her wedding day. Among those things are: "The groom did not show up," "We can't find your dress," and "The best man lost the rings so we're going to substitute Ring Pops." A smoking generator doesn't make the top fifty.

"We're a go! We're a go!" the other coordinator yelled into the headset. I raised my arms before the band with the pomp of an orchestral conductor. Music lifted into the air as the chandeliers glowed to life overhead and the caterer fired up the grill. Marital crisis averted.

Sometimes, Ash, in life, as in weddings, you just have to figure it out as you go. And sometimes the moments when it all goes wrong—the moments when you must divert the generator from exploding lest it set the tent on fire—actually become your fondest memories.

Entrepreneurs

One of the things that inspires me most about you is your entrepreneurial spirit. You have a way of approaching the world that is so unique and entirely your own. This is creativity at its finest: connecting dots the world does not see. You bring a new vision to problems that others get stuck on; you see over fences and around walls that get in everyone else's way. Mix that with your constant desire to innovate and create, and I can only imagine where you'll go.

Entrepreneurship makes the globe go 'round. And more than that: after so many years in the NGO world, I've come to the firm belief that entrepreneurial business is the most powerful driver for lifting communities out of poverty and minimizing vulnerability to exploitation. Our team realized this a few years into our work at Not For Sale and transitioned much of our focus to job creation.

The fact that you want to start a business and develop a vision that will bring opportunities to many is thrilling. I laughed when you told me you thought it wouldn't make a big enough impact. Nothing could impact a community more than having the opportunities—as you and I have so abundantly had—to contribute to the world around them. As I recently heard the great businesswoman Marilyn Carlson Nelson say, "The best philanthropy is a job."

I will, however, add one warning.

The curse of the entrepreneurial heart is that you will never be satisfied. Entrepreneurs are never content. That's what makes them entrepreneurial. The very restlessness that drives you forward will be the same angst that keeps you up at night. Entrepreneurship is both a fire igniting and a fire consuming.

Be aware of this, Ash, as you embark on new ventures. You'll be tempted to think that success, that the finish lines, will relieve you of your angst. But the reality is, for people like us, the journey is where the joy of work is worked out.

The Roller Coaster

When I was your age, I wish someone had told me that vocation is like a theme-park ride. That knowledge alone would have saved me countless days of overzealous worrying when plans fell apart and my emotions took their lowest dives.

You see, if you embark on an entrepreneurial project, one where you seek to create and make an impact, then you're agreeing to get on the roller-coaster ride.

It will have high highs and low lows, so don't be surprised. *This is a roller coaster.* It said so on the sign. You will invariably climb into the clouds and then drop so suddenly your stomach flips, and you'll be so close to the ground you could reach out and touch concrete. But you will come up again, because this wild journey is a ride.

I was shocked by this reality when I began work in the non-profit world. I would be elated as we chugged up and up toward the heavens, high on possibility, and then gutted when something tremendously exciting would fall through. My emotions would go plummeting to the ground. But after a few years of this, I finally began to anticipate the ups and downs. It was all part of the process. The anticipation alone allowed me to keep a peaceful core in the midst of manic circumstances.

Of course, some people's rides are slight rises and dips, while others are chock-full of loop-de-loops. Somehow, I always seem to find myself on the latter. Whatever level of risky ride we choose, our stomachs will inevitably drop. That is, unless you sign up for the cave train ride that circles the park around everyone else's roller coasters. But even then, a dinosaur or two may pop out to surprise you.

Weaving Together

As you can imagine, most people made fun of the contrast between my work—slavery and weddings—and I would usually laugh with the groomsmen about it until they started equating the two. But I also wondered at times how these random roads of work would intersect. I genuinely had no idea.

One autumn we hosted our first Global Forum on Human Trafficking, bringing dozens of speakers and hundreds of participants together from all over the world. Midway through, I realized I knew how to use an event to create a life-changing experience for the attendees. I knew how to incorporate lights and sound and space and special touches to make the time emotive and memorable. It wasn't the marrying of two people, but it was the marrying of a larger community to the shared vision of a movement.

Throughout the years, we planned more forums and luncheons and galas. We put on gatherings for some of the most influential people in the world—tech founders and billionaires and celebrities and all-star athletes—and each time my coordination skills kicked into high gear to serve our organization's purpose.

What I know now that I did not know in my wedding planning days is that when you pursue the things you love doing and direct them toward causes you care about, eventually those skills and passions will somehow weave together. And the final weaving may surprise you.

I spent too many hours pondering what all my odd jobs had to do with each other, instead of trusting the journey as it worked itself out.

My time behind a deli bar taught me to listen to people and get the details right. Waitressing on summer breaks taught me to serve and give people grace. (I was known to bring Long Island iced teas when someone just wanted regular iced tea. Waitressing was never my forte.) My internship in Brussels taught me international affairs and office dynamics, and wedding planning taught me how to bring people together and make a gathering meaningful. Strangely and beautifully, all of it made me a better anti-slavery activist.

Who would have thought?

The Last Wedding

I'll never forget the last wedding I did.

It was Palm Springs, a perfect fall night. The lights were dimmed to a shimmering glow and stars ignited the sky as guests danced away on the hotel deck.

I was in the corner, exhausted, feet aching, looking frazzled and very non-J.Lo. A few guests filtered by asking about the cake-cutting time (no judgment: I always ask about this too), and one conversation transitioned into small talk.

"So, how long have you been coordinating weddings?" she asked.

I walked her through my short career, and as I did I had a revelation, friend. I didn't want to be talking about weddings anymore. By this point, I had been coordinating on weekends simply to supplement my income from working at an NGO—because, contrary to popular belief, nonprofit startups are not the fast track to a life of financial success. In that moment, it wasn't just because I was tired, or because one too many mothers-of-the-bride had drunkenly screamed in my face that she couldn't find the guest book and it was all my fault and how dare I ruin *her* special day. But as this guest and I talked about the bad DJ and the amazing cake and the overall success of the evening, all I wanted to do was stop the conversation and tell her about what I really cared about: my day job, fighting slavery.

I turned away from the light conversation that night with a new resolve: I wasn't passionate about weddings anymore. I had been, but something in me had shifted. I'd been coordinating for almost three years at that point, and what once thrilled me had become a burden. More than that: I wasn't excited to answer the calls of girlfriends who were newly engaged to discuss their peony varietals. And I *love* peonies! I was okay with being tired and even burned out, but I wasn't okay with being jaded.

I had always taken comfort in having a backup career of wedding planning. If we miraculously solved the global problem of slavery and put ourselves out of business, it was liberating to know I had a skill I could make use of. But at that moment, as the guests danced the Electric Slide, I realized my heart wasn't in it. I still think wedding planners have a dream job, but it was no longer *my* dream job. I never planned another wedding after that.

Feel Better

Darling Ash, I love the idea of you heading to Cape Town this summer. And what a perfect organization for you to work with! I have friends in South Africa I cannot wait to connect you with. I think your time at the Willows and your experience organizing so many of your fellow students to serve will prepare you well for this experience.

And hey, I'm sorry you weren't feeling great when we met last week. I meant to message you after, and then I forgot. I'm sorry, sweetie. There must be a bug still going around. I'm sure you're through the worst of it by now, but you should see the campus doctor just in case.

Love you a bushel and a peck and a hug around the neck.

Always,

X A

PS—Let me know how you're doing, regardless.

Quantum Potes
Tantum Aude.
(As much as you can do,
so much dare to do.)
UNKNOWN

PART IV

SENIOR

CHAPTER 18

ON JOURNEYS & RESTING

Most people have that fantasy of catching
the train that whistles in the night.

WILLIE NELSON

SEPTEMBER 4

Dear Ash,

You've made it to senior year!

I can hardly believe you're here. Didn't you just begin this wild journey? I loved every detail you wrote about Cape Town. What a beautiful, challenging, transformative couple of weeks. And speaking of journeys, oh, do I have stories to tell you.

But first, I'm sorry I never wrote to you in July. This summer has been crazy and strange and unusual. But, as I've heard it advised, "Never ruin an apology with an excuse," so let me just say once more that I'm sorry for being a less-than-dependable friend.

Get Away

Some seasons in life we have to stay, and sometimes we have to move.

Some days, Ash, we just have to get away.

After leaving Not For Sale this summer, I knew I needed a detox. I hadn't had a vacation in almost six years. I mean, I *had*—trips here and there and weekends away and such—but I had ended up working every single time a car or airplane dropped me somewhere new. I would tell everyone I'd be overseas with my away message on, and then inevitably someone would email and insist the need was urgent and a new email blast must be created. I would cave and stay up half the night reformatting the template. Part of it was our organizational culture. Rest was not one of the team's core values. But the other part was that I wanted to be needed. It's an addictive feeling, really. Beyond that, I wasn't mature enough to know how to say no.

I'll never forget one of those days when the exhaustion all compounded for me. In the course of a month, I planned an event for high-power European executives in Amsterdam, visited my host family in Brussels, finished cowriting a book, coordinated and cohosted our annual global forum of eight hundred people, and then flew down to LA to put on a massive launch event and concert that was filmed for a reality show. Which, thankfully, never aired, so don't try to Google it.

Those events sound exciting when I read them back now, but the memories are clouded by exhaustion to the point of despair. Working until three a.m. each night in Amsterdam, sobbing in a heap on the bathroom floor when my laptop deleted the manuscript, and coming home shaking after the global forum only to repack and fly out for another event the following morning. I hadn't eaten and was so physically and emotionally exhausted that my roommates walked in at ten p.m. to find me bent over the stovetop, eating soup straight from a pan. I was too exhausted to pour the soup into a bowl.

We can sustain insanity for a time, but I had tried to juggle too much for too long. It was only by sheer grace that I didn't have a meltdown.

And that's how I ended up in the middle of the largest food fight in the world. A tomato fight, to be specific. Because when I left Not For Sale, I decided to take a sabbatical.

The Road Trip

The tomato fight was entirely my cousins' idea. Bradley and Samuel are about the best travel mates you can find. Both are in the military—Bradley in the army and Samuel in the marine corps—so they're organized and adventurous and resourceful. When you get pulled over by a police officer looking for bribes in Montenegro, these are the guys you want to be driving with. The even greater benefit is that they grew up in a family of six sisters, so they understand the importance of dressing up and having doors opened at restaurants and why you might need a few extra minutes to get your eyeliner just right. Plus, they've got terminal cases of wanderlust and a white fedora named Bruno who makes his way into every photo on every epic journey.

I needed to get away, and Bradley was stationed in Europe, so when they asked me to join them on a road trip, the answer was an obvious yes.

The boys picked me up in Barcelona. They had everything planned and researched with just enough room in the schedule for daring detours. First stop: the world's largest food fight.

It was the middle of August, but for some odd reason a cold front had hit the south of Spain. There we stood, shivering in T-shirts and goggles and clutching our phones in clear sandwich bags. The town stirred to an eerie silence as locals shuttered their windows and the chattering from the crowds quieted to an anticipatory lull.

Then they came. Like war machines into a sea of soldiers, a caravan of dump trucks rolled down the streets of this tiny town and stopped, in unison, to tip their burdens to the sky.

Out into the street poured fourteen billion tomatoes. Or close to that, I couldn't count. The air was silent a moment longer as several thousand young pilgrims took in the sight.

Thump, I heard. Then, *thump, thump, thump!* A tomato hit me in the back. Then another grazed my head. The battle had commenced.

Within minutes we were drenched. Not in a cheery, cartoonish rouge like I'd imagined, but in an orange, acidic slop of tomato innards. My goose-bumped skin sizzled and burned. Within minutes the streets were flooded with tomato guts, a river of soup that came up to my knees. At one point I tried to take a step and my flip-flop dislodged from my foot, so I dove in on all fours to grab it. My cousin caught my arm as I began to slide away.

"I think I'm done!" I yelled, six more tomatoes flying past.

Driving back to the hotel on plastic-bag-covered seats that evening, I could hardly stomach the stench of my skin and clothes and crusted hair. There's a reason people use rotten

With my cousins, Bradley and Samuel, in Spain at the world's largest food fight.

tomatoes as a way to show dislike. We pulled off at a rest stop to change and tied our battle-soaked T-shirts into plastic bags like they were dog litter. I thought for a moment about saving mine, then chucked it into the bin.

Sometimes, Ash, at the end of the day, you just have to live things out. To ride the wave of anticipation, marvel at the experience, and survive the acidic stew. You have to hide from the strangers with arms like major-league pitchers and get a photo amid the mayhem. You have to take it all in and then leave it behind and go forward with a story to tell.

Always and eventually, every experience must end. Whether it's a job that you loved or the sun going down on a wonderful day. Always and eventually, it is time for the next journey to begin.

The Drive

Montenegro is a long way from Germany, and so most of that Eastern European road trip was, as road trips often are, in the car.

We flew from Barcelona into Munich to pick up our shiny station wagon and drove all night on the Autobahn, the boys drinking neon European energy drinks and doing pushups on the roadside to wake up at four a.m. We got lost and found and were utterly exhausted, hitting Croatia at dawn where we jumped into a waterfall. From there we made our way south along the snaking coastline roads to Montenegro, a region once known as one of the most glamorous tourist destinations but largely forgotten since the war. We took the ferry to our hotel, explored empty towns, and watched a movie at midnight atop a castle on the ocean cliffs. Bruno in tow, we donned our best James Bond attire and found a casino. It wasn't *Casino Royale*, but it was close enough for us. The locals stared us down with a shaken mix of suspicion and curiosity as I won big on a game of roulette. My lucky number: twenty-two. We used the winnings to buy a steak dinner.

But the best part of the trip, Ash—the part I wasn't expecting to love—was the drive. The process of getting to anywhere we were going. Bradley at the wheel, Samuel riding shotgun on DJ duty, and me in the backseat watching the scenery slide by. Sometimes we talked about life or the landscapes, sometimes we sang along to Lorde or Lana Del Rey, and sometimes we just sat in silence for stretches of road.

In that silent space—the silence I usually filled with emails and calls and to-dos back home—my mind wondered and marveled and wrestled and was at rest.

Silence began to restore me.

Listen

Ash, given everything you told me this month, I'd encourage you to spend some time alone. There is so much you will miss if you don't take moments to get still amid the busyness. Moments to stop talking, and to listen.

Do you remember my bedroom in my apartment in San Francisco? Did you see the word that sits over my doorway in chiseled gold letters? *Listen*—my daily reminder. It's the first word I look at when I wake up each morning, and the last thing I read before bed every night. Listen to God, listen to others, and listen to your heart. Listen before you speak, and hear what the world is instructing.

At the time I put it up, I'd somehow gotten my hands on a box of large ornamental letters during a Restoration Hardware sale. *Hope*, *love*, and *joy* were each too short a message to stretch across my door frame. *Peace* was spoiled by the fact that it used a letter twice.

The letters above my door. My daily reminder.

And then it came to me: *listen*. In a quiet moment, there was my word. Not only was it an impressive *six* distinct letters, but it was a word that I'd never thought much about. I considered how much I needed to hear it. Every day.

For people-people like us, the best times to listen are when we're alone. Our souls need this time, this silence, like our bodies need water. Aloneness refreshes us, cleanses us, and lifts us. One of the greatest failings of our connected world is the lack of listening, because there's always another something to steal our attention.

At any given time we are all feeling so much, and if we don't get away on our own, we will never be quiet enough to hear what those feelings are telling us. We run from our pain to find relief and fail to see there are lessons in the angst. In the biting cold air is a message about discomfort, in the hunger of our bellies is a metaphor for need, in the questions of our conscience is a chance to rethink our actions, to repent, to seek forgiveness. In the grief that presses against our solar plexus like a crushing hand is the opportunity for future empathy—for opening our eyes to our own story, and the stories of others, to be molded by them.

Yet in each of these sensations we have the tendency to escape. At least I do. My default is to turn the water up hotter, to stuff my belly with a snack, to blast the music so loud I can't hear my thoughts, to surround myself with a hundred boisterous people so drunk on their social lives they can't feel their own pain.

We miss the messages when we don't get quiet. When we don't listen. When we don't lean into the discomfort and feel.

Limitless

I know how busy you are, Ash, but you need to get sleep. At the risk of sounding parental here, it is essential to your health and well-being. To your clarity of mind and good decision-making. I've never heard you sound so utterly exhausted, and I'm worried for you. I don't like the thought of you barely getting out of bed this weekend.

The better rested you are, the better things seem. As you become fatigued, you are more likely to look on the dark side of things and worry more, which hurts your test scores. Remember that Shakespeare quote we love about "sleep that knits up the raveled sleeve of care"?[1]

For years I pretended I was fine on limited shut-eye. "No rest for the wicked," I would exclaim in my delirium, bragging about the four hours I'd gotten the night before. "I'll sleep when I'm dead." And I genuinely meant it. The only problem is, such lack of sleep will only make the living less abundant. More than that, it limits our productivity.

I've told you before that I used to pride myself on being busy. Especially in college, and then even more so in the years directly after. Busyness was my badge of significance.

I've heard it said that we can only work eight productive hours a day. This is not including breaks, but rather the *truly* productive hours. Can we work longer? Of course! Are we very productive? Well, according to the study and barring the super-human among us, not really.

If I'm honest, I think this is probably true. The days at work when I had to leave by five to make a dinner or event, I often surprised myself with my own productivity in the hours before I departed. I knew I had a hard stop, so I accomplished more per minute. The days when I had nothing and stayed late, barring a pre-event all-staff blitz, I was usually sluggish and inefficient.

We're better with our time when we know there's a limit and commit to work within it.

There is a beauty in boundaries, dear girl. Our culture fights against them, but there is liberation inside limits. Imagine a pasture with no fence, a garden with no edge, a river with no riverbed, an ocean with no shore.

I have found that the happiest people I meet are usually the ones living big within their boundaries. They place limits on their money, their time, their relationships. Rather than fight the limits of their ability or location or family or what have you—they expand within them. They excel despite, or within, or because of their boundaries.

Limitlessness will not satisfy the aches within us, Ash. To be honest, I almost wish that wasn't true. Because if it wasn't true, if more of everything could satisfy us, it would mean I could make a plan. I could amass all the money and things that I could with the absolute certainty that those possessions would land me in a place of peace. But, for better or for worse, I know that they won't.

Joy is found in contentment. Satisfaction is found in wanting what we already have, and in accepting what we don't. It's painting with the colors we've been given, rather than complaining about our palette.

Sacred Rest

This brings me back to the topic of sabbatical.

When I first moved to San Francisco, I was working on writing a book for my friend and pastor, Britt. Anxious to prove to my nonprofit bosses that I wasn't about to fall behind on my workload, I made a point to work harder, to stay later, and to always be clocked in. It was madness, in retrospect.

Upon moving to my new city, I realized I would never be able to keep up with the friends and family I already held so dear, so I made two commitments: The first was not to date anyone. I couldn't wrap my mind around having a relationship amid that workload. Sorry, boys. And second, I wouldn't seek out new friends in San Francisco, but rather focus on investing in the precious friendships (and family, of course) that I already had. It sounds a bit pathetic as I write it now, but I was so overwhelmed that I could not imagine adding one more thing to my life. Nor could I bear the thought of letting down people whom I loved.

A few months later I was sitting in my church in San Francisco. I was tired and generally burned out. More than that, I was resentful toward God. I felt like I'd been working so hard to serve in every way, and all I had to show for it was exhaustion.

Dave, my pastor in San Francisco, began speaking about that Sunday's topic: sabbatical. I yawned and fidgeted. I knew it well enough. Then Dave started to lay out his case, and suddenly he had my attention.

Dave explained that thinking we can do it all, and not resting, is actually an act of rebellion. It's saying to God and the world that we alone are capable. To not give a day back to God and consecrate it for rest is to not recognize that it is by God's grace that we live and move in the first place.

What hit me was how unproductive I am whenever I don't properly rest. Some weekends I would arrive home on Friday evening from work, write nonstop in my pajamas, and not leave the house until Sunday night for a trip to the grocery store. I would find myself listlessly staring at the same paragraph, or the same blank page, for what felt like hours on end. It was like my brain had gone on strike to boycott the inhumane working conditions.

I was convicted. If I'd only been faithful to rest, honoring the hours rather than sucking the life out of them, not only would I have enjoyed the process more, I would have also been more efficient. I thought back on the night before the book was due, when I sobbed in a heap on the bathroom floor. Maybe it didn't need to be that way.

Maybe, if I'd rested, I wouldn't have built up this calloused resentment.

Sacred rest, I realized, is of sacred importance. Maybe that's why it's in the Ten Commandments.

The Magic Word

I am amazed that you are taking on so much this semester, Ash. It's remarkable. And it's probably also why you're exhausted.

Personally, I'm learning more each day that one of the most important lessons of adulthood is learning how to say no. What a small but powerful word. When my brother turned two, it was the only thing he cared to say. "Honey, would you like the red cup or the blue cup?" "No." Isn't it ironic that it's the word most quickly forgotten in our busy, stressed-out, much too grown-up lives?

The ability to say no is, in part, the difference between people who are successful and people who are just busy. Our culture uses *busy* as a crutch, and I catch myself using it all the time as a way to validate my worth in the world.

"Hey, Allie! How are you these days?"

"I'm good!" I reply. "Really good. I mean, *so* busy."

They look at me sympathetically, with a twinge of admiration at my importance and my martyrdom for humanity, and I feel a little bit proud and a little bit phony. Was I really busy today, or was I checking Facebook while procrastinating on my emails? Probably both.

Yet somehow, the simple fact that my time is occupied makes my life feel just a little more worthwhile.

This trait has followed me since childhood. My parents called me "the go-for-it girl." Was it happening? I was in. This is an excellent trait if you're running for mayor of a small town, but not so much if you're trying to live a healthy and whole adult life. One that includes exercise and sleep and intentional *rest*.

I call it busydom—"busy martyrdom"—the tendency to sacrifice myself on the altar of always doing something, as if my constant doing could somehow save the world.

A few months ago I attended a conference where Kay Warren spoke. Amid discussing her global work with orphans, she paused to herald the merits of saying that magic, two-letter word. And not giving any excuses when she did it.

Someone would ask her to attend an event, or host a luncheon, or meet with their group next Tuesday at three, and she would simply thank them and say, "I'm sorry, I can't." And leave it at that.

They would wait a moment for her excuse—international travel? A speaking engagement? A different event they might be invited to?—and when she would offer none, the conversation would simply move on. "People don't need an explanation for every no," she urged us. "A simple no is no enough."

That permission hit me like a snowball on a sunny day. I was allowed to say *no*. And more than that, it was possible to do so graciously. Here was a woman I admired, doing great and important social justice work in the world, who'd been able to accomplish so much simply because she knew when and how to politely decline.

She knew how to create space for things that matter most.

As the scion of the investing world, Warren Buffett once said, "The difference between successful people and very successful people is that very successful people say no to almost everything."[2] I suppose this self-made billionaire knows a thing or two about getting things done.

I was venting to my friend Kyle recently about my propensity to say yes to all that's asked of me. And he challenged me to try a new framework: if the answer isn't "absolutely yes!" then the answer is "absolutely no." I realized, for the sake of my life and my health and my sanity, I had to stop saying yes to the maybes.

When it comes to spending your time, Ash, wisdom is about knowing when to say a firm and confident yes, and how to gracefully decline everything else. Declining so you can have space to say yes to the very best offers when they come.

Walk with Me

At the height of that harried, hectic season, I caught up one evening with my friend Dan.

Dan is a maven in the music world, managing rock bands and music festivals and producing shows. In the nineties he was an associate manager for U2, and Bono introduced him to my boss, knowing their shared commitment to social justice and the poor. Dan loved when his artists and music festivals could support our work, and it was in the context of this work that I came to know him.

Dan has circled the globe and seen it all, and he loves to

shatter people's worldviews—especially mine. He likes to say the awkward or uncomfortable or hilarious thing that makes you think differently about your perspective.

We stood outside that dark night at a dingy music venue, the bass thudding against the stage door, and the smell of spilled beer and cigarettes drifting into the street. As always, I was talking shop: going on and on about the impact we were making and the campaigns we were launching and the events we were hosting and the places we were going . . . until finally, Dan stopped me midsentence.

"Allie," he said, with the slow, warm tone of a father, "someday you are going to die."

I looked at him, confused.

"And you are going to get to the gates of heaven and Jesus is going to meet you there. He is going to welcome you in and take your hand in his and he's going to say, 'Allie, you sure did a lot for me. You were constantly going and constantly serving and constantly working. I saw that. Thank you for that.

'But now it's my turn, Allie.

'Now I want us to do something that I have wanted to do with you for a very, very long time . . .

'Let's go for a walk.'"

I have never forgotten Dan's words that cold night. They haunt me like a melody as I run and run and run, rushing and working to serve a God who desires that I would just be with him.

A God who is waiting to go for a walk.

Checking In

School sounds like it's been extra tough this semester, and I know you have exams coming up. I'm praying for you, cheering for you, Ash.

Are you still going to see Dr. Martin tomorrow before class? I'm eager to hear how the test goes. I'm eager to talk to you, in general. Don't wait to write. Just call me after, will you?

And promise me you'll rest. As my grandma used to say, whatever trouble you're facing, "It will all look better in the morning."

Now sleep—

x

So we beat on, boats against the current,
borne back ceaselessly into the past.

F. SCOTT FITZGERALD

CHAPTER 19

ON HOPE & FIGHTING

I know a cure for everything: salt water . . .
sweat, or tears, or the salt sea.

ISAK DINESEN

NOVEMBER 2

Ash,

I—I can't—I still don't know what to say. Oh, Ash, my sweet Ash.

I'm reeling from our call, still wrapping my head around your voice telling me the news. Of what Dr. Martin said, of what this last test showed.

Cancer?

Ash, you're too young to have cancer. You're too full of life and opportunity and wonder to be shackled by disease. I don't understand why. None of this makes sense. It does not make any sense.

I don't understand cancer. Its myriad shapes and forms of malady. Sometimes easily curable, other times not. I am going to read and study and work to comprehend everything I can about what is going on inside of you. What I understand the least about cancer is why it happens. Why the cells that burst forth life within us suddenly turn against their home.

You are so brave, my darling girl. I would not have the calm or grace or elegance in facing this the way you do.

Ash, you said to keep the letters coming, but I don't know how right now. I don't know what to say. Nothing feels normal or right.

And yet, I know you'll get through this! I know you will be so much stronger, so much more *you*, for having lived this story.

The Beauty Mark

I've known too many friends and family members who have battled cancer, who have looked that devil square in the eyes and done the tempestuous dance with him in a hospital gown. Most have lived through it; a few have not. But all have come through victorious, somehow. Victoriously healing, or victoriously letting go.

Christie had cancer a few years ago, Ash. Did I tell you that? She had skin cancer.

She was planning to move to New Zealand with a missions group called YWAM, believing that the season ahead would be the most significant spiritual journey of her life. She was right: it was. But not at all in the way she intended it to be.

Months before her trip, Christie's mom took her to have the little beauty mark just above her upper lip looked at by a dermatologist. Christie had noticed the little mark growing for about a year, and at first she loved that tiny mole because she thought it was seductively Marilynesque. But it had shown up somewhat overnight back in her days of modeling and frequent tanning-bed use, so she finally started to worry.

The dermatologist biopsied the mole, and the cells came back cancerous. *This is inconvenient*, Christie thought. The dermatologist insisted the mole be removed, but said it would be a very simple procedure with minimal downtime. To Christie, it was another to-do item to check off her list, something to handle in between finding voltage adapters and travel shampoo.

At her mother's urging, Christie returned to the doctor a few weeks before her flight, a bit nervous about the procedure, but praying she'd be out of there in less than an hour. She was totally unprepared for what was about to happen.

The surgeon cut into the mole, slicing back the first layer, then running it under a microscope to "make sure she got everything." She hadn't. So she went in with the scalpel again.

And again. And again. And again.

Each time, Christie had to return to the lobby and wait for the doctor's verdict. Five times the surgeon went back. To cut again, to dig deeper, to carve away more of Christie's lovely face. Six hours later, Christie had such a gaping hole that the surgeon was forced to carve all along the corner edge of her lip, detaching and then stretching her skin to meet the other edge.

The result was gruesome.

When I got to Christie's house, her face seemed to have doubled in size, swollen and bruised, buried under the layers of gauze crowning her head. She couldn't open her mouth, couldn't eat. And she would vomit through her swollen lips from the nauseating effects of the pain medication.

"I'm fine, I'm fine," she mumbled three days later as I sat with her on the couch, my heart breaking at her agony.

Then she wandered into the bathroom to shower, and I bristled at the muffled sound of an agonized scream.

Ministry Training

Christie never made it to the sparkling coasts of New Zealand. But she did get six months of ministry training. Half a year of the most difficult spiritual journey of her life.

You see, Ash, Christie would tell you that for most of her life she had based her worth on the way she looked. This was only exacerbated by men who dated her for her appearance. The modeling industry had made her feel pretty, but never pretty enough.

In the six months after her surgery, her face remained contorted. Half of her mouth couldn't smile, and the scar stretched around her lip and toward her nose like a sickle.

In that first week she wandered out to the supermarket one afternoon, determined to buy her own groceries. The checker stared at the bandages encircling her head and chin.

"I hope it was worth it," he smirked, assuming plastic surgery.

"I had cancer!" she mumbled, storming out before he could utter a wide-eyed apology.

As horrific and painful as that season was, Christie calls it her season of heart deconstructing—of soul healing. She had no guarantee her face would look the same, no hope that anyone would ever want another picture of it. Slowly, surely, she let the love of her appearance wither and die.

And slowly, like snow sliding in icy sheets off a roof when the winter sun comes out, Christie began to decouple her identity from her appearance.

Her story has a beautiful reconciliation. But, Ash, I am struggling to reconcile your cancer with faith, in the same way I've struggled amid the illness of every loved one through the years. I struggle because I love having answers, and right now I don't have any. Only questions and worries and fear.

I don't know why we have pain like yours, Ash. I really don't. I only know that God is with us in that pain, and if we're lucky, it transforms us.

Metaphors We Choose

Already I'm referring to your cancer as a fight, as a battle.

My rhetoric professor at Westmont, Dr. Spencer, would make us reflect on the ways in which we deploy metaphors like this. The way, for example, we talk about time like it's money: "We spent time together; I need to save time."

And the most prominent cultural metaphor he cited? You guessed it. How we approach cancer: a battle, a fight, something you can beat (which you will!). His point was that we make cancer even scarier and more powerful than it ought to be by elevating it to the language of war.

Given that, I'm going to try to change the way I talk about this disease: acute lymphoblastic leukemia. I'm going to call it your ALL. This is greater than your battle; it's your journey. It's your ALL.

Actually, it's *our* journey.

All of us—your friends, your family, your school, even the Willows community—will be walking through this beside you. We'll be giving your ALL our all.

Honest Pain

I want you to know, Ash, that you don't have to be "okay" through this. You say you are, but you don't have to be. You don't have to keep it all together. It's okay to be broken in front of me, in front of your family, in front of your friends. There is strength in shared brokenness. Communities become whole when we allow our burdens to be collectively borne.

I went through a rough patch during the fall of my sophomore year. Adam had fallen ill again, this time worse than the last. It was another rare disease that no doctor could seem to diagnose. A nightmare déjà vu. Our family was watching him waste away once more. Later that fall I would draft an email to my teachers, preparing to miss my finals in case I had to go home to say good-bye. We came perilously close to losing him before a doctor took interest in his case and prescribed an unusual drug with a side-effect that managed to save his life.

In the midst of that, after an agonizing decision, I broke up with my boyfriend, Chris. Do you remember me telling you about him? He was my first date, my first kiss, and then, my first heartbreak. Ending it was the right decision, but I was crushed. I felt like I'd lost my best friend.

I lived between two alternate universes that fall. In one, I was the happy, overactive student leading a dorm of twenty-four freshman girls as an RA. In the other, I was a devastated mess. Frightened about the future of our family and what lay ahead, and reeling from the loss of my relationship.

Every week that year our resident director, Mark, would have a one-on-one meeting with each RA to check in and see where we needed support. That afternoon we'd grabbed smoothies from Blenders and, in a response to a question about how I was doing, I downloaded a censored version of my hardship. I explained the situation by emphasizing why everything was really, actually, all okay! No cloud, all silver lining.

We were lumbering around the Coast Village Road roundabout in his vintage powder-blue Mustang when Mark finally interrupted me midsentence. "Allie," he said intently, eyes on the road, "it's okay to hurt."

I was silent.

"You are going through an incredibly difficult time, and it's okay to be honest about it. You don't have to pretend like everything's all right."

I nodded, lip quivering. No one had ever given me that permission. Or maybe I'd never given it to myself.

"You will minister far more to the women in your section if you are real with them in your pain than if you pretend to have it all together."

I nodded again, slowly.

"I want to challenge you to be real with them. I want to challenge you to just . . . hurt."

A few days later we had our weekly section meeting—Testimony Tuesday, as we called it, because someone would share her life story each week. I'll never forget that evening, as I sat on my pale green duvet and divulged my messy story with those young women. Honest, raw, real, *hurting.* I broke down in tears, and they huddled around to comfort and console me. I felt so loved.

In the days after, most came to thank me for sharing my heart with them. I received handwritten notes under my door, expressing how much it meant that I would allow them into my pain.

I was moved, deeply. And then something even greater happened, Ash. I can't describe it really, except to say the dynamic in our section changed after that night. There was more honesty, more connectedness among the girls. There was a love that existed between us, a sense of support and safety I hadn't picked up on before. We were one community in a way we had not been before.

I believe one of the deepest human desires is to be known: by others, by God, by ourselves. But often we avoid true knownness, running about in a thousand misdirected ways. We think people want to know the best version of ourselves, the okay things, when really all they want to know are the truest parts.

We can only be known by others so far as we open ourselves up to them. What we hide, hides us. And what we share shows others we love them enough to trust them with our stories.

The Flames

Today I went back to Westmont, Ash. I strolled around the campus and wandered through the oaks and sat on a bench below Kerrwood Hall, processing the news of your cancer. Then, as I always do, I went to the chapel.

It was only three years ago that fire blazed through the hills of Santa Barbara. Hungry and vengeful it spread, lit by the remnant embers of an innocent bonfire some university students left burning in the hills. Those hills were as dry as tissue paper that summer, and in an hour they'd erupted into flame.

I was working from DJ's house in the hills that evening, back when we were still dating. He was traveling for work, arriving home that night, and I wanted a quiet place to hammer through a project.

The winds had picked up and were blowing their warm, familiar gusts through the sycamore trees. But this night was different. The wind felt sharp and brutal and unfriendly. I sat on the deck, my phone dead, working away against the dim light of my laptop. Someone walked along the street below me swinging a flashlight across the road, which I thought was strange. A giant gust blew a deck umbrella over and I ducked as it came hurtling toward me. I grabbed my computer and scurried inside, the house completely dark.

I was on a deadline, so I kept working, plowing away at my document. Someone knocked hard on the front door and I jumped, but then I heard them run back up the steps to the street. *Must be a neighborhood kid.* I shrugged and kept working.

Fifteen minutes later a door banged open in the basement and a man came running up the stairs. I caught my breath.

"Allie!" It was DJ's best friend, Deyl. "Allie, there's a fire. Get anything valuable. We have to go."

I leaped into action, grabbing hard drives and journals and a few random things. It's so strange what you take in a moment like that, salvaging pieces of someone else's life.

The house sits on a steep hillside, and as we ran up the steps to his car waiting in the driveway, I saw the glowing red wall of flame rising across the street. Bright and hot and ethereal, like a strange and terrifying dream. The kind that jolts you into waking and leaves you shaking in cold sweat. Except this was not a dream. We sped down the road, past burning brush and trees, thick ash littering the windshield and clouding the seaside air.

Much of Santa Barbara burned that night.

I stood alongside the ocean an hour later, staring up at the hills. I watched the fire snake its way along the California Riviera, consuming trees and homes and memories. I watched it edge against the house where I'd just been.

Half of the homes on DJ's street burned that night. His was spared, but only because a friend who worked for the local electric company had managed to check on it, spraying fire retardant on the ground and hosing off encroaching flames that lit the trees like torches.

Westmont burned that night as well. Students were shuttered in the gym as fires crawled across the campus. Not a soul from the school was hurt, but when flames engulfed the oaks around the chapel, our hearts were crushed. That tiny white chapel was the heartbeat of our school. We could endure knowing that parts of the campus were damaged, but the thought of the chapel being consumed felt too difficult to bear.

I slept at Deyl and his wife Paige's home that night, giving our apartment up to students. The city felt dead and alive all at once. Dead in the destruction, yet alive in the sense of one-ness and community that emergencies often bring. I never loved Santa Barbara or its people more than when we went through the fire together.

When the sun came up the next day, my friends turned on the news. The reporter announced that somehow, miraculously, the Westmont chapel had been spared, and—for just a moment—in the midst of all our sadness, it felt like Christmas morning.

I went back to the chapel this afternoon, as I do with every Westmont visit and anytime I'm processing the heavy parts of life. I go there to sit beneath the wooden beams and pray and listen and tap out old hymns on the piano by the windows. The surrounding trees are still charred and bear the scars, but new growth is breaking through. The land is barren, but its heart beats strong.

Somehow, in some way, I think hardship refines us, Ash. Amid the pain, these seasons have the capacity to prune us.

Hard things have the potential to cut away the overgrowth and strip us to our core and make us feel ugly and barren and raw. And that pruning allows the brilliant, strengthened life to burst forth. The same way a fire may cause years of damage but centuries of new life.

The Westmont chapel.

Josh Newton

I choose to believe, amid such hard things, that God has not abandoned us. More than that, I choose to believe he is with us. That he is nearer now in our sorrow.

The Dirt

You are one of the blessed unlucky ones who experience the harshest of trials so young in life. Unlucky because of the pain, but blessed because you have the chance to know a depth of life and human experience we can only touch when we suffer.

Ash, I am awed by your grace and your hope, by your courage and your calm. I feel like I—and your parents and Emma, and Peyton and Amber and all your friends—are taking this so much harder than you are. Tell me, where does your peace come from? How could you still get us laughing in the midst of all this?

I'm beginning to believe that each time we come through something difficult or risk something great, or experience something that makes our spirits sing, the genie of our true selves comes farther out of its bottle. And it can't go back. We can't compress the bigger self that now exists back into a smaller space. This journey is bringing you into a bigger self, dear girl, so much bigger than you even knew was available to you.

You are a gem, Ash. You are teaching me every day. I have never seen the beauty of your character glow more brightly.

And you know what? We'll get through this. One day, one chemo treatment, one radiation therapy at a time, we will crawl and claw and clamber our way through this storm. Our greatest impact often comes through our lives' greatest brokenness. Trees and grass and wildflowers grow from messy dirt, not perfect concrete. Sometimes our hard places must crack open so living things can break through.

We don't get to choose our trials, but how we respond to them becomes our story.

You are strong, and I know you'll be stronger for this. I just hate the pain you're in now. I would do anything to bear that pain for you. I wish so much that I could.

We are with you, darling girl. You are never alone. And, most important, you are loved.

So very loved.

X

The marvelous richness of human experience would lose something of rewarding joy if there were no limitations to overcome. The hilltop hour would not be half so wonderful if there were no dark valleys to traverse.

HELEN KELLER

CHAPTER 20

ON PAIN & SURVIVING

The world breaks every one and afterward
many are strong at the broken places.

ERNEST HEMINGWAY

FEBRUARY 4

Ash,

This letter is late, and I'm so sorry. I'm sorry for a lot of things right now. I'm dictating these words and editing with one hand, arduous, painful, slow. Like everything in life right now.

Thank you for your messages, for thinking of me so much while you yourself are struggling so. How are you feeling this week, brave girl? Much braver than me, I think. Your plight is so much more serious, yet I feel so much more defeated than you seem to be.

I know you are wondering what happened. This has taken me a few days to compose, as I can only do a little at a time. But it's good for me to write you the story. It's something productive and focused to do.

I'm here in my new home now, New York City. I thought I would hit the ground running, but instead, I just hit the ground.

The Premonition

It happened after the World Economic Forum in Davos, where heads of state descended in helicopters and Mercedes-Benzes on a tiny mountain town in the powdered-sugar Alps of Switzerland. They stomped through the snow to panels about the world's ailments, then drifted to country-sponsored cocktail receptions and violet-lit corporate after-parties with terrible music and dazzling strobe lights that pulsed across the new-fallen snow. If you haven't founded a multibillion-dollar company, you can usually procure a hotel pass for a hundred Swiss francs that grants you access to some of the side goings-on. I came with my colleagues and my boyfriend, Ben, and slid past prime ministers in the halls. It was all very surreal and exciting.

Human rights leaders and rappers and industry titans alike find a voice in the annual magic and mayhem of Davos. No matter your title, you too will don snow boots and slide here and there on the ice—perhaps the most democratizing element.

The whole show of it is overwhelming and invigorating and
inspiring. The mountain air and
altitude of ideas had me on a high.

Until it happened.

It's strange, Ash. I had a pre-
monition. I feel funny writing it
to you now, because I can't say I
believe in premonitions. But I told
my mom, on multiple occasions
before going, that I was afraid of
snowboarding in the Alps.

"I really want to go," I'd say,
"but I just don't want to fall and
break my arm."

My view down on Davos,
Switzerland, just before the fall.

Even my mother thought that was strange. I'm not one for suspicion and am pretty gung ho when it comes to adventure. But for some reason, I kept saying I was afraid of getting hurt. I'd shake it out of my mind, but I meant it. Never in my life had I broken a bone, but if there was ever a time to break one, it was certainly *not* then.

For one, I had the trip of a lifetime in front of me. I was supposed to join Jeannie on a friend's excursion in Morocco the following week. Ash, you know how much I love the Middle East. And ever since my cousin Rachel spent a month in Morocco when I was a teen, I've had it at the very tip-top of my bucket list. I was going to wander the streets of Casablanca and the markets of Marrakesh and ride—you guessed it—on top of camels in the desert. Morocco would be my last great excursion before a new season of work and city living set in, and I was ready.

Which was another reason I could not get hurt: I was mid-move to New York City. My sublet on an apartment would start the week after I returned, my entire life having been shipped from San Francisco in a seven-by-eight-foot container, now stored somewhere in New Jersey.

And, of course, there was work.

I'd just started working with a new company that invests to upgrade supply chains in Asia and had plans to travel the following week to shoot the documentary I've started producing. Everything was building to a critical moment. This was my last great adventure before life got serious.

I could not get hurt.

The Fall

It happened slowly, Ash, like a championship replay, and as fast as a barrel of gasoline bursts into flame.

I had just come through a dodgy stretch of mountain pass on my snowboard and was gaining confidence. I'm a water baby, having grown up on the coast, and I hadn't hit the slopes in a number of years. I was rusty, yes, although I'd never been good at snowboarding in the first place. It was a dreary day, the falling slush blurring my goggles in a grim and foreboding haze, but the slope stretched out in front of me, flawless. I made my way down the hill tentatively, picking up speed. Then more speed, and more speed.

Too much speed.

Suddenly it felt as if my board was hydroplaning above the slope, a bald-tired car careening on black ice. Left foot forward I turned to carve, desperate now to slow down. The right edge of my board caught the snow as if it were concrete, and my body exploded forward, feet whipping above me in the air. My left hand went down instantaneously, protecting my neck from breaking the fall.

The snap was audible. An explosion of bone that rattled the gears of my soul. The force whipped me back into the air, then landed me flat on my back. The world split in shocks of light around me, like a fist shattering glass. I heaved and gasped and choked for breath, and then I wailed. Blubbering, fear escalating, panicked.

I later learned from my surgeon in New York, Dr. Barron, that it was a burst fracture. Sketching on a scrap of paper, he explained that the radial bone of my left arm had shot like a torpedo into my elbow socket, exploding into multiple chunks of bone that were floating, unattached, in my arm.

A Swiss rescue worker in a candy-apple red jacket skied me down the mountain. I went headfirst, on my back, strapped to a board that slid behind him until we were met by an ambulance at the bottom. I remember thinking at one point, as I watched the trees whip past overhead, that this could be a fun ride in another universe or time. A place without pain and breakable bones.

The doctors in the emergency room spoke limited English and offered even fewer facial expressions. When the X-ray proved unsatisfactory, they sent me into a special room with a young CT scan technician who looked at me tentatively as she stood before the looming white mechanical tube.

"I'm going to need you to, uh—" she measured her words— "straighten your arm all the way flat and hold it in the middle of the machine."

I cradled my arm like a baby, staring as if she'd just asked me to let the ambulance drive over it.

"Or you could lie on your back and hold it straight out behind you," she offered, demonstrating.

I was shaking uncontrollably from shock, but the horror of that backward option filled me with a newfound grit. I walked to the machine, grabbed my wrist, and ripped my forearm away from my body.

Sobbing, gasping, screaming. "Please, just do it!" I shrieked, when she hesitated in front of the machine. I may have sworn at the poor girl too. I honestly can't remember.

But the worst pain was yet to come.

The Journey Back

It took three trains and two flights to make it back here to New York. I had begged the stoic doctors to do whatever surgery they needed there in Switzerland, holding tight to the vision of myself in a cast on a camel in Morocco. But they shook their heads in unison and told me I would need a lot of follow-up care and should go back to the States, my bones disconnected in rubble. I didn't even know if I should go to California or New York. That week I was, technically, homeless.

The doctors handed me three prescriptions to pick up before I left. "Level one"—they pointed to the German names—"level two, level three."

"Level three," they added, "is for the airplane." Apparently, everything swells. A lot. I was petrified at the thought of travel, more afraid than I've been about anything in my life.

On the train the next morning I watched the tiny Swiss towns go by, life-size versions of the ceramic Christmas scenes my aunt sets out each December. I kept blinking, shaking my head. This was a dream. It had to be a dream. I had to go back and undo this, undo that fall and that turn and that mountain. I sat there, stunned by the permanency—that I could not unwind this. I could not knit my bones back together, and yet only a veil of time existed between my present moment of brokenness and those seconds before the fall.

I looked down at my legs, which were quivering uncontrollably. Shock had kicked in again.

Take Courage

We say "take courage," Ash, because it's something that is always just before us—like the bar of a trapeze swing hanging over the hardships below. These moments are opportunities to jump out and grasp tight onto courage and hold fast as we swing over the world and its paralyzing fears.

I think most people are surprised by suffering, but suffering is a part of the human story. We may experience heartbreak if we love, and loss of the things we treasure most. Yet we are never as rocked as we should be by the horror of what another went through after they've survived it. We think, *Of course they survived, of course there is redemption.* But when it happens to us, when we are in the darkest depth of the pit, everything looks different.

The apostle Paul wrote to the Roman church: "We also glory in our sufferings, because we know that suffering produces perseverance; perseverance, character; and character, hope. And hope does not put us to shame."[1]

Character is like playing an instrument, Ash. We must find opportunity to practice it again and again, lest we get rusty and forget how to play. Because, when the moment that matters is before us, our response puts that character we've developed on full display. A character wrought most through hard circumstances.

To be truthful with you, I don't feel God's presence here in this trial. I don't feel any purpose. I'm so clouded by the fear and the pain. I am choosing to believe that all shall be well, because I know no other way through this. I would say that I'm clinging to hope, but it's more like I've let go of everything. I'm letting hope wash me away.

I wish desperately I could be by your side right now, Ash. To be in constant pain from my accident is difficult enough, but to be grounded from flying and unable to be with you through this round of chemo is more difficult than I can bear.

I heard from Emma how you've made so many friends in the hospital. The nurses and the doctors and the other patients all blessed by your infectious laugh, your stories, your joy. A joy made only more real as it suffers.

There is a special kind of Japanese pottery dating back to the fifteenth century where the artist takes a dish that's been broken and transforms it into a one-of-a-kind work of art. Have you heard of this, Ash? It's called *kintsugi*. The artist repairs the pottery with fillings of gold and precious metals, making the broken places a part of its aesthetic, a part of its story. Not surprisingly, the end result is so much more beautiful and unique than the original was before breaking.

I hope, someday, I feel that way.

The Pain

Ash, there are, I think, two ways to experience pain: to fight against it, or to move with it. To let it hit you like a wave and wash over you—to feel it with every fiber of your being.

When I first got back from Switzerland, my sweet momma flew in from California and met me and Ben at the airport in New York City, where I'd decided to have the surgery. We drove straight to the emergency room. The ER did more excruciating X-rays and then sent us away with a surgeon referral. I was stunned. I'd been told by the Swiss doctors that I had three days to have the surgery before permanent damage would occur. And here I was driving away, no better off, in even more fear. What if we couldn't find a surgeon?

We spent the next day on hold with every orthopedic office in New York. "Call them again," I would cry to my mom, as we listened to another rejection from a cold receptionist. Finally Dr. Barron, one of the best in the business, saw my CT scans and, thinking it would be a challenge, decided to take the case.

"I'm booked tomorrow and gone next week," he said as we sat in his office, "but if you don't mind a seven a.m. surgery, I'll cancel my rounds and do it Friday morning." I nodded vigorously and my mom nearly collapsed in relief, all of us squinting back tears.

When they wheeled me into the operating room at dawn two days later, I practically leaped onto the cold silver table. I was so overcome with the fear of losing movement in my arm that surgery seemed the greatest saving grace.

As nurses positioned themselves around the operating room, the anesthesiologist pumped a clear liquid into my IV. She smiled. "In a moment, this is going to feel like you've had a couple of cocktails." She looked like someone I would want to get cocktails with. I tried to respond with something witty but my words slurred, and then I was under.

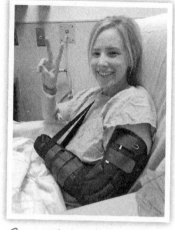
Going into surgery.

I woke up hours later, my arm back in the sling but completely unfeeling. An eight-inch wire tube ran inside my chest, where they were dripping anesthesia over a bundle of nerves to numb any feeling in my left arm. During extreme surgeries, maybe two or three a year, my surgeon said, they leave this catheter in, attached to a device pumping continual anesthesia. This, it turned out, was one of those cases. The risk of infection was high, but the risk was outweighed by the chance of me feeling the aftermath of the surgery.

As I came to, Ben and my mom were beside me explaining Dr. Barron's enthusiasm over the success of the operation. I would later learn, via pictures he'd snapped midsurgery on his cell phone, that he'd expertly extracted the large broken shards of my radial head and laid them out on a table. Most surgeons would have sawed off the rest of the bone and inserted a prosthetic, something that would need to be replaced every decade. Dr. Barron, however, was at the top of his trade. He proceeded to drill and screw the pieces of my bones back together, inserting them into my arm with a metal plate and seven surgical screws. The girl in his office two days before had told me about these screws.

"They're one thousand dollars each," she exclaimed, "but we'll waive the cost with the surgery." *Buy one surgery, get seven screws free.*

The Worst

Barron was elated at the success of this surgical feat. I was given painkillers and sent home. I felt strange and my numb arm felt stranger, but I had made it through the worst.

I thought.

Just before ten that night I sank into a deep sleep, only to be awakened an hour later by a feeling unlike any I've known—or would ever hope a person to know. I gasped, lunging forward on the couch in terror.

It's difficult to describe pain of a specific magnitude, Ash. It felt as if someone had dipped my arm in kerosene and lit my bones on fire. It felt like my elbow had been locked in a vise cranking tighter, and tighter, and tighter.

I screamed like I've never screamed before. My groggy, sleep-deprived mother came running. She calls it her dark night of the soul, and I can imagine that seeing your child in so much pain would be almost worse than experiencing the pain yourself. *Almost.*

Every few seconds the pain would escalate, and I was thinking it could not possibly get worse—then another agonizing wave would crash against me. I was delirious, hyperventilating.

Let me be clear on one thing, Ash: I have never yelled at my mom. Many teenagers have, and I understand that, but yelling was never our thing. Also, you've met my mom so you get it. She is some epic mix of Mother Teresa and June Cleaver, just not the sort of person you yell at, even if you're in high school.

But that night I yelled at my mom. I screamed and begged

for something, anything, that would stop the pain. I would have let her chop the whole arm off if I thought it would quench the searing fire in my bones. At one point I looked down at my forearm, certain it was going to explode. Or else I would die. There was just no way I, or my arm, could sustain this mounting, explosive pressure inside.

My mom, meanwhile, was panicking. Shuffling through the four hundred medical papers we'd accumulated, unable to find any number to call. "Call 911!" I shrieked.

In the ER they shot me full of morphine, which I now liken to manna from heaven. Within five minutes the pain subsided. I could breathe, and think, and survive. Turns out, the anesthesia pump had malfunctioned. The anesthesia that was supposed to numb my arm for the next three days had never pumped into my chest and down that eight-inch wire tube and over my bundle of nerves. The ER doctors treated this like an unfortunate inconvenience, as they tweaked and fiddled with the fanny-pack pump on my hip.

I've never given birth to a child, but after that night I think I could handle it.

At a Ten

This week I saw Jeannie. She was just back from Morocco, and as much as I longed for her exuberant energy and her comforting words and the stories of her journey, I braced myself for the visit.

I should say, Ash, I feel selfish complaining about anything in comparison to what you're going through, even though your prognosis is rosy. But you wanted the story and the details, so I will share them.

By the time Jeannie arrived, I was staying at a friend's empty home at Astor Place while he traveled overseas. The towering white columns framed a view of the New York City skyline, reminding me I was still not at home in this place. Everything I owned was in that storage unit in New Jersey.

Jeannie came bursting through the elevator doors carrying a vase of white roses, and we laughed when she determined that my green and yellow arm was the size of my thigh. It was so good to see her.

"So." I swallowed, head flopped back like a mop on the couch. "How was it?"

Jeannie's face got serious.

"Do you want the 'one' version," she asked, "or the 'ten'?"

You see, a few months earlier, Christie had given birth to my godson, Christian, and Jeannie had accompanied me to the hospital for a visit. Christie's husband, Will, came to the hospital corridor to meet us, where Jeannie squealed in anticipation.

"I am just so excited for this!" She was practically levitating as we washed and sanitized our hands. "I've never seen a newborn baby before!" She looked like a puppy that had caught the scent of Thanksgiving dinner on the table.

Will was quiet, then spun around.

"Jeannie," he said, stopping us in our tracks. "You're at a ten. I need you to take it down to a four." He turned back around to lead us down the hallway, and we skipped behind—muffling laughter.

Now Jeannie was asking me the same. What energy level of story did I want? For a moment, I almost said level one. Could I bear to hear about the trip of a lifetime I'd missed? To hear the tales of journeys I did not have and adventures I did not embark on and the glamorous parties I did not attend?

Yes. Yes, of course I could. But not because I was so magnanimous. It was because I was so darn curious.

"Ten," I replied, determined.

Jeannie's face erupted into fireworks of emotion. She proceeded to tell me about camel rides through the desert, dancing in the ancient streets, winding corridors leading to private residences scattered with roses, palatial baths and silken Egyptian sheets and personalized mystery notes each night detailing thoughtful encouragements to the receiver. The insanely generous host? A friend of ours from the Middle East, who wanted to bless her community with the trip of a lifetime. A blessing I had not been blessed with.

I giggled at the stories and marveled at the pictures, and I meant every awed word of enthusiasm. The trip looked incredible. I was happy for her and the others who'd attended. But when Jeannie left that night, I wandered slowly into the back bedroom, plopped down on the bed, and let out a sob.

I think I cried for a solid five minutes. And when I say cried, I mean I let the waterworks go. I flung open the doors of my own little room of self-pity and slowly strolled the perimeter, corner to corner.

Once all the dull glitter of my sad pity party had floated to the floor, I decided there wasn't much more that my tears could accomplish. In the darkness of pain and silence, I stared at this lonely, imagined mental space of mine, with its make-believe Polaroid snapshots of all I had missed in Morocco, and everything I would miss through my recovery. Then I took one last sniffle, a long, deep breath, and that was that. I knew I would have to accept that this injury and this pain and this missing out were part of my story.

I hate not getting to choose my story.

The Silver Box

Before Jeannie left that evening, and before my self-pity settled in for a nightcap, she handed me a silver box about the size of my hand. The surface was inlaid with an Arabian design, and the inside held a velvet core full of dried rosebuds.

Jeannie explained that on the day they rode camels through the Moroccan desert they'd rested for tea in the shade of a cavernous tent. The theme of the trip was roses, and there were scatterings of dried rosebuds decorating the entire place. Jeannie gathered the group together and told them about what had happened to me—my story, the break, the surgery. She gave each of them a rosebud and asked them to say a prayer for me as they held it.

This box, which she'd found in the Marrakesh markets, contained each of those two dozen rosebuds—the realization of which made me cry.

Sometimes, that's all we get, Ash. We don't get our dreams, our adventures, or our health. Sometimes all we get is a silver box of dried flower prayers. It is beautiful and it is hard and it's a treasure. It's not the treasure we wanted, but it's enough.

I'm sorry for not being there for you right now. At least, not in the way I wish I could be.

Send me stories from the hospital, will you? We'll heal through this together.

Forever,

 x

Of one thing I am perfectly sure:
God's story never ends with ashes.
ELISABETH ELLIOT

CHAPTER 21

ON DARKNESS & HEALING

I've loved the stars too fondly
to be fearful of the night.

SARAH WILLIAMS

MARCH 31

My dear Ash,

Day by day the snow is melting, and I am healing with it.

Dr. Barron says it's miraculous, the rate at which I'm mending. Arm shaking, I did a push-up at the hospital today to show off. He says he's going to share the details of my procedure when he speaks at conferences.

My physical therapists keep pushing me too, willing me to get as much movement now as I can. It's excruciating, the mind-splitting pains of healing that come with each visit, several hours every other day. As with any great trauma—emotional, physical, or spiritual—I'm realizing we cannot heal alone. I don't think we're meant to. We need another's hands to work the muscles and twist the bones and take us to a place of mending we couldn't find alone.

I'm hurting, but hopeful.

Yet, as I grow whole, you seem to grow sicker. I'm scared for you, Ash. I'm not sure I believe you're so very okay. I heard the strain in your mother's voice, the burst of tears on the call from Emma. There's a stillness in your speech that wasn't there before.

I have my ticket now, and I'll be there in just weeks. May will be our month of healing: your chemo wrapping up, my arm bending at the elbow again. We'll stroll down State Street and walk along Butterfly Beach at dawn. We'll buy dinner from the farmer's market and walk through the olive trees, and eat mint ice cream at San Ysidro Ranch beneath the stars. Have I taken you there? They grow their own mint in the garden and let it marinate in milk all morning beneath the perfect sun. It tastes like joy—bright, cold, sweet—and is made all the sweeter by the host of dancing fairy lights in tangled branches above.

We will heal, and I will take you there.

City of Doors

I'm missing Santa Barbara and its sweetness, its salty air, its sycamores, its warmth.

New York is different, a place of hardness. Concrete and metal, buildings with sharp angles, cement with decades of dirt ground in. I feel off-balance here, as if I might fall again. And if I fall, there's no soft earth to land on. Sinatra sang if you can make it in New York, you can make it anywhere. I always thought that sounded inspiring. Now I wonder if it's eerie too. What about the ones who don't make it?

"I confess I find New York rough and strange," says Jo March in *Little Women*, "and myself strange in it." That's how I feel at this moment, Ash.

The girls here dress differently than they do where I come from. They wear all black and walk in high boots on the right side of the sidewalks like commuter lanes. The avenues smell of perfume shops and falafel trucks and garbage left on the street to decay. It is a city building up, and tearing down, and building, building higher all around you. I find myself craving space. Inner space and outer. Space between people, space in my room, space to see the stars.

And yet, amid the madness, New York is magic. Every possibility is here. I hate it and I'm intoxicated by it, all at once. Every time I want to unearth the suitcase from under my bed and catch a flight to California, New York romances my spirit and inspires my thinking and I fall in love all over again. It's a dysfunctional relationship, yes, but maybe there is purpose in this dance of dysfunction.

Manhattan is a city on a grid. It's a community of every culture, the capital of the world. For years I've taken three-day business trips here and been swallowed by the mess of streets and blaring horns, but now it all makes sense. If LA is the city of dreams, then New York is the city of doors. Everyone is knocking on something or looking for keys, hoping, one day, that some door will swing wide before them. Eagerness and hope fuel the hustle of this place.

Ash, you must come visit me in New York. After the mint chip ice cream, we'll get you on a flight to JFK to see the city. I'm praying your second-choice job option becomes your first, because I know how much tougher you are than me. You'd thrive out here. You were made for this city, dear girl. This city, with all its opportunities and wonders and absurdities, was made for you.

Our Scars

I've been thinking a lot about scars, sitting here staring at mine.

Our scars tell our stories. They speak of our brokenness;

they sing of our healing. There's an ancient Chinese proverb that says, "The gem cannot be polished without friction, nor man perfected without trials." You and I are well-polished gems now, don't you think? Someone ought to make a crown out of us.

I'll admit it, though—I'm pretty tired of being polished. On days like today, I want my dullness back. I miss who I was before the hurt made me deeper and stronger and more understanding of the sorrows of the world. I don't want to go back, but I miss who I was before I knew this pain that I cannot unknow.

You've had an indomitable spirit through all your trials, Ash, and I'm awed watching you. Through the good days and hard ones, your joy is constant, even when tempered by pain. Pain I *know* you are bearing, and I know you're not telling us about.

I'm trying to stay in good spirits, too, but I'm struggling. I'm mourning the fact that my arm will never work like it used to. Close to it, I hope, but it will never be the same. It will always be part metal, part engineered and reinforced. It will always have been broken, once it mends. We can't undo our hurts. We can only live beyond them.

On my better days, I'm reminded of how entitled I feel. To health, and strength, and an arm that bends. I had them once, but they were never promised to me at all because they're gifts. And the lack thereof only reminds me of my frailty and humanity and how very blessed I am.

But that's on my good days. On days like today, I find myself waltzing with self-pity. And my, is he a terrible dancer. I'm ready for us to get some quality time together, Ash, so I can remember how to keep my chin above the waves. Like you.

So to Speak

Enough on pain. Let's get down to business.

You will do spectacularly on this speech, dear girl! *Do not be afraid.* Just be the brilliant, wonderful you. I'm so proud.

Honestly, Ash, I can't understand why you're nervous about this when I know how wonderfully you'll do. What a good skill to perfect at your age! Most people are more afraid of public speaking than they are of dying, which already makes you leagues beyond the general populace for simply agreeing to do it.

A bit of advice: I want you to get out of your head, so to speak, because this speech is not about you. *This is not about you.* Say that to yourself—post it on the bathroom mirror and repeat it like a mantra. Public speaking gets scary and awkward and awful when we turn our whole attention on ourselves. The diatribe that can start in our minds is a death trap.

Oh no, everyone is looking at me. Where do I put my hands? On the podium. No, that's awkward. At my sides? I'm so thirsty. Oh my gosh, I haven't said anything yet. Where are my notes? Oh no, my hands!

Ash, imagine if you entered every conversation you had obsessing over how your face looked and where your hands were and overthinking every word you were about to say. Do you do that? Of course you don't. Because you're comfortable and confident with people. And because you genuinely care more about how others are feeling than you do about yourself in those moments. That's why you talk to people in the first place.

This is what you must do with your audience, dear girl. Think more about the crowd of graduates and families than you think of yourself. You're just a conduit for the baccalaureate message, and overthinking *you* will only get in the way. It would be like driving a car somewhere but only focusing your attention on how the car looked and the sound it was making rather than on the road, your directions, and your destination. Of course there is a time to shine the hubcaps, but once you're driving, you'd best keep your hands on the wheel and your mind on where you're going and just enjoy the journey. That's your reason for driving in the first place.

Once you've put the feelings of your audience first, public speaking is easy. And fun. *Really* fun, because you can read the room's energy and feed off it. Or, in this case, the auditorium! I always try for a little humor to break the ice, the way you'd crack a joke with a friend. Say something they don't expect; be sarcastic or self-deprecating! Laughter will open a room faster than the pearly gates swing wide before a saint. "Laughter," says Anne Lamott, "is carbonated holiness."[1]

I actually prefer large audiences. I really do. When you affect laughter or reflection or an "aha" moment in your audience, it's magic. When they're with you, it's intoxicating. Like a synchronized flash dance that you get to lead. And even if you stumble or, God forbid, fall, the music will continue playing, and your partner, the audience, will still be beside you. Laugh and keep going, along with the melody. We all are amateurs here.

Like I've mentioned time and again, people will remember how you made them feel. And *you*, my dear, make everyone around you feel alive.

Your mom says there will be a ramp, just in case you need the wheelchair. Or your sister and I can walk you up, if you prefer. Oh, this will be so special, Ash. All of us will be there, cheering you on, with all our hearts.

Out of all the students at your school, your classmates and teachers chose *you*, dear girl. You! For your courage, your tenacity, your spirit, your joy. For the way you inspire us all.

Have I said that enough, Ash? How enormously proud of you we are?

All Shall Be Well

I moved into my apartment last month, my room at the top of a six-floor walk-up in Nolita. The name means "North of Little Italy," although it's so high up I feel north of everything. Those six flights of stairs seem treacherous now, but I'm making it. I have a snow-covered balcony overlooking Elizabeth Street, where tourists marvel at the shops below and locals chat over green juice and designer kale salads on yellow chairs outside the Butcher's Daughter. Mine is an old building, but a magical perch—a tree house in the city heights. If I tilt my head just right, I can see the Empire State Building from my bed at night.

It's been difficult to unpack things; I can only move my arm a little. I've made my home amid cardboard boxes, like a child's dream fort. The pain of healing is ever present, the slightest movement still excruciating. Like most old New York apartments, there is no central heat, and with this sling it's been impossible to wear sweaters or long sleeves. Only tank tops with jackets draped over my shoulders. I shiver in my room all night, motionless in pain, willing the space heaters to fill the room with warmth.

But day by day—slowly, surely, in fits and starts—the winter and the pain are melting.

The first things I unpacked were my sheets and blankets. *Warmth.* There's a pillow on my bed now that my mom gave me for Christmas, handmade

All shall be well. Jeannie's box of roses is up there on the shelf.

by her dear friend Ruth, an artist and calligrapher. It's a large, cream-colored tweed thing stuffed with down, perfect for leaning up against. Elegant black letters fill the front and whisper their words when I glance toward my bed: "All Shall Be Well."

My mom has a smaller version of the pillow, and I'd loved it. I mentioned I wanted one a few months back, when all really *was* well. How ironic that the day I unpacked it in New York, to christen it among the pillows on my bed, my world was anything but well. Lately I've felt so unwell I want to cry. But each day we go on, and the phrase somehow rings true.

These were the words of Julian of Norwich, an English anchoress and Christian mystic of the mid-fourteenth century. From an isolated cell she prayed each day to know more of the nature of God. In her youth she became very ill, to the point of death, and was administered her last rites. As she lay on her deathbed that afternoon, she dreamed a series of revelations in the midst of heightening pain. Her near-death experience was also her gift to the world.

As Julian cried out the question, "Why must there be suffering?" she heard the voice of God saying, "All shall be well, and all shall be well, and all manner of things shall be well."[2]

At this, she felt the peace of the world, a peace that came with the knowledge that whatever our temporary suffering, someday all will be put right.

Someday all shall be well.

Promise Me

Ash, your graduation is coming soon! So soon—just weeks. You are so close to freedom, to the world beyond. You'll be twenty-two, at last. A working woman when this job comes through. And cancer free, when the transfusion succeeds and these chemo treatments are done. I have a really good feeling about this new guy who's been calling and visiting you. We haven't even talked about him yet!

There is so much to celebrate, so much to look forward to.

I'm already planning your party and—I wanted to surprise you, but I just cannot wait anymore—it will be at the Willows! The entire community has been coming together to make decorations and cards and little handmade gifts for you. Everyone loves you so very much. Even cranky Charlie, who could not crack a grin if the joy of the human race depended on it, has managed to put a little something together for you, Ash. I think you're the only person who's ever gotten through to that cantankerous man, I swear it.

I figure since it will be both your birthday *and* your graduation that month, and since you've come through so much this semester, you are due for a real celebration.

You need to know how much we're all anticipating the chance to celebrate who you are, dear girl. To reflect on the impact you make, every day, on all of us. Even when you're at the hospital or at home, healing.

My window box in Nolita, with the first sign of spring breaking through.

Promise me you'll pretend to be surprised about your party, will you? Promise me you won't give up. Promise me you won't let go of joy. Promise me, Ash. Promise me. We need you.

Today I looked out the window of my Nolita apartment and I saw a sprout. Yes, one single sprout, in the old planter box that sits empty on my balcony. One tiny burst of green broke through the clods of dirt. When I look out my window, it gives me hope. Tiny, bright-green hope.

I can't wait for all that's ahead. For you, for your life, for our friendship, for all your relationships, really.

This has been the hardest time of our lives, but dawn will break.

It always does.

X

All shall be well; and all shall be well;
and all manner of things shall be well.
JULIAN OF NORWICH

CHAPTER 22

ON COMMENCEMENT

Hold loosely all that is not eternal.

A. MAUDE ROYDEN

MAY 16

My darling Ash,

I know you'll never read this, but you've forever changed my life.

I'm shaking as I write these words. Last words. An infinite hollow place aches in my chest and rises to my throat, concrete slabs pressing my lungs between sobs. My mind is numb, yet feeling everything. My eyes are red and dry as dust, but tears still come.

I'm off the floor now, breathing deep. I spent the evening there, curled up on the carpet, hearing my heart's beat, remembering you. Images flash across my mind like slide shows: running in the rain beneath the Golden Gate, that August afternoon on the harbor, the window table at Jeannine's where you asked to share my breakfast and these monthly letters, your face thrown back to the sky in joy. I can no more dam this flood of tears than I can stop the stream of memories, so I let them all crash against me, one by one.

Sorrow tastes like salt, and gasps of air, and nothingness.

Today would have been your twenty-second birthday. A day that's always felt, to me, like a destination you were moving toward. As if the building momentum of these last four years—of your last twenty-two years—would come crashing into a glorious commencement.

Happy birthday, beautiful girl.

Our Miracle

We were all there by your side when you left us. Eight days ago now. I still did not believe you were slipping away, not until the last hours, the last moments. I wasn't ready to lose you, no matter what the doctors said that week. I still believed every miracle was possible. Even as the transfusion failed and your body wasted away, you were so alive! You had to live, Ash. There was no other end to your story.

When I got to the hospital, Emma met me at the door, and I knew instantly that everything had changed. I felt my knees give way, but they must have carried me forward, because then I was in your room. The doctors and nurses stepped away. Your father grasped your right hand in both of his, and your mother gently stroked your face. Emma curled up beside you on the bed, her arms around you tight. Everyone was holding on, as if you could still be pulled back to us.

We held your hands as you breathed your last. Aching, reverberating, slow. Each ragged gasp a dagger in our hearts, cutting the cords that held you to us. We sang together, your favorite hymns, just like you asked. Just like you wanted. Emma, tucked beside you, wouldn't stop holding on. She stayed there long after you let go.

You died on a Friday morning, your favorite day of the week, at 11:21 a.m.

I will never forget the image of that room. You were beautiful, and yet you weren't *you*. I don't know how else to describe it. The color that lit your features, the vibrancy that made you stand out in a crowd and drew people to you, had drained from your face into some distant place. Your skin paled to a pastel hue, your lips turned grey, the sweet grin gone. Still you were our Ash. And yet . . . everything that made you Ash—the spirit, the soul, the life that animated you—had moved beyond that place.

I know now that we had to let you go. You were ready to let go, long before we were.

I screamed at God from the driver's seat of my rental car. I screamed and cried and called him names you would have scolded me over.

"Where was the miracle?" I sobbed, my hands against the dashboard. "Where was our miracle?"

And in that silent space, I realized it was you.

You were our miracle.

Knowing you, Ash, was the miracle all along.

Honoring You

Twelve hundred people came to say good-bye this afternoon. The sun came late, and warmed us. It was a celebration, Ash, in every way. It was a petals-falling kind of day.

Darling girl, you would have loved it. You would have drunk each moment in. I caught myself twice as I turned to see your face light up and realized, with a start, I would never see those sweet features again.

But we remembered you. We sang and laughed and cried and cried and cried. It looked like a wedding from afar—adorned in bright daisies and wildflowers and garden roses, each friend carrying a stem for you, Ashley Rose.

Your teachers said you learned with passion and zeal. Peyton and Amber and a dozen other friends shared stories and memories and wisdom from your adventure-filled days. We laughed hard, and cried harder. Dozens flew in from your hometown, a few from Cape Town too. The front row was reserved for wheelchairs—your friends from the hospital to whom you'd brought so much joy and, of course, the residents from the Willows. More of them than I could count. They gave heartfelt remarks, some struggling to stand, taking the mic to simply say they loved you and sitting down again in labored breaths.

We honored you, Ash. Because knowing you was an honor to us all.

In the Ground

Ash, I need you.

I need to hear your voice telling me with grace and gravity that all of this will be well. I need to tell you about this friend that I've lost, this light that's gone out, and the darkness that has settled in her place. Every place that you touched knew growth, color, joy.

I never realized how much I need you, Ash: how much I've learned from you, how much you've shaped me and showed me who I want to be. All I want to do right now is call my sweet friend and share the burden of this searing pain, but you will never be there again to answer.

Ash, you have changed us—every one of us who brushed up against your light.

I do not understand death. Nothing could feel more unnatural. The pain in my spirit exceeds anything I've ever known. I pleaded with God in that hospital room to keep you with us. And then, by your side, to bring you back. Darling girl, how did you have so much peace as you went?

Your body's in the ground now, beneath packed earth and living things. The world blossoms around you in the peak of spring, and we are growing too. From knowing you. From the thousand tiny ways you nurtured us.

Twenty-Two

Ash, I have so often failed at finishing well, but here for you, postmortem, is my promise kept: your twenty-second letter.

I planned to write this month on commencements. On why we call the graduation a beginning, rather than an end. But your commencement ceremony was a memorial—a celebration of who you are, a marker of your eternal beginning.

Every day from now we will battle between the suffering of losing you, and the gift of having you with us for the twenty-two years that we did.

Thank you, Ash, for sharing your journey with me. It has been a gift I will cherish and carry until the day I meet you on the other side, where tears have no place, and joy has no end, and I will know the warmth of your light once more.

Thank you, Ash, for being.

Love without end,

X

All that is gold does not glitter,
Not all those who wander are lost;

The old that is strong does not wither,
Deep roots are not reached by the frost.
From the ashes a fire shall be woken,
A light from the shadows shall spring;
Renewed shall be blade that was broken,
The crownless again shall be king.

J. R. R. TOLKIEN

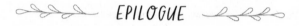

EPILOGUE

i carry your heart with me
(i carry it in my heart).

E. E. CUMMINGS

SEPTEMBER 1

Dear Emma,

It's been more than three months since Ash left us, and I miss her more each day. I can't imagine how you're bearing this grief, as close as the two of you became. Even in moments when you didn't get along, I always knew it was only because you are far too much alike.

Your sister loved you wholeheartedly—more than you could ever hope to know. So much of the way she lived was rooted in her desire to be an example to you. She wanted to be the big sister she needed at your age.

I can only imagine how proud she'd be now, seeing you begin college today.

So much of who Ash is lives on in you, Emma. Her winsome spirit, her wise heart, her way of loving people. You carry forward the very nature of her life, walking a path she went before.

For that, I know she would have wanted you to have these letters. In hopes they would be a light for your journey—that is, as Ash knew, the destination.

Write to me when you arrive?

With love,

X

ACKNOWLEDGMENTS

There is a beautiful South African concept called *ubuntu* that means, "I am because you are." This word captures the way I feel about the small tribe of people who have made the story of *Twenty-Two* possible.

This book *is* because of them.

First, I want to thank my publisher, Thomas Nelson, for taking a chance on me. Thank you, Jessica, for believing in me enough to advocate for this book. Thank you for so thoughtfully shepherding me through the journey, and for your wisdom and discernment in editing. This would not be the book it is without your expert touch. Thank you Aryn and Tiffany, for being such passionate advocates for this story. A huge thanks to my copyedit team, Brigitta and Jocelyn, for caring so well for every detail of the prose and catching every "tyop." Thank you to the design team for laboring over the cover and creating such a whimsical image to communicate the message of this book. I love it. And thank you, Vik and Cubby, for your creative support in the process. I am so grateful for your friendship.

Thank you—so much—to my agent, Lisa, and the team at Alive Literary. Lisa, I could not have imagined this journey without your guidance and mentorship. You saw in me—and this story—something worth believing in, and this book exists because of your belief.

Writing is a creative process, but it's a physical process too, and I'm so grateful for the many people who've created space for this project to come to life. Thank you, George and Joan, for allowing me to write, so many times, from your beautiful home in Water Mill. Your support has been the greatest gift, and the stories in this book will always remind me of the chair by the fire and the afternoon light in the barn. To Summerly, for taking me in when I didn't have a home, and for letting me wallpaper your West Village apartment with notes and outlines throughout the editing process. I love what we did with the décor. And thank you to the Voge family, whose flat in London is the place where I first woke up with this idea and committed to write the book. Your hospitality has forever inspired me—literally.

Thank you, Jeannie, for your wisdom and your zeal, and for helping me live life at a ten. Thank you, Jonathan, for the constant camaraderie and counsel through this writing process. Seriously—what would we have done without each other? Thank you, Leif, for your creative partnership and your constant belief in my abilities. Thank you, Esther, for being in my boat.

Thank you to Dave and the entire team at Not For Sale— from the staff and the board to the volunteers and the supporters. We grew up in this movement together, and we built something incredible in the process. I'm so grateful for the journey we shared through those years. I'm also grateful for the support of the Freedom Fund, and for all my friends and comrades in the anti-slavery movement and the social justice space. There's no greater honor than working on behalf of the good of others, and how fun that we get to do it side by side.

I'm daily thankful for my tribe of friends, from Santa Cruz to Santa Barbara, Los Angeles and San Francisco to New York, and all over the world from there. You are beloved, and you make this wild journey the joy it is. I'm grateful for each and every one of you and the stories we share. Thank you also to many of you for letting me share those stories here. I apologize if I forgot to warn you first.

Thank you to Westmont College, for being home to the four most transformative years of my life and for helping me become a lifelong learner. Thank you to Nexus Global Youth Summit, Praxis Labs, and Creative Visions for being communities of such great inspiration. Thank you to my Wedgwood Circle family: Amy, Mark, Jacob, and Hae-Jin, Good Lit, and all our members, for being my community of creative support throughout this project. Thank you for spurring me on toward excellence as we work to make good, true, and beautiful things together.

Thank you to my church communities: Twin Lakes Church, Reality Carpinteria, Reality San Francisco, and Trinity Grace Church Tribeca. You are my family. To the pastors who've counseled me and the communities that have worked faith out with me: thank you for the infinite ways you've supported me and showed me the way of Jesus. You have taught me how to love well and to serve, and so much of who I am has been shaped by doing life together.

Marge, you have been a grandmother to me, and the legacy of who you are will forever live on through those of us who knew you. I'm so thankful I could read you some of these words before you left us. Thank you to the other mentors who have modeled life and faith for me, and the young women who've allowed me the privilege of speaking into their lives. Your questions are the reason I wrote this book.

Thank you, Britt and Kate, for the central role you have played in my life and this story. For teaching me about love and loss and hope and grief. The character of Ash was inspired by the life of Daisy Love, and I hope more people get a glimpse of who she was because of it.

Thank you, Christie, for being my sister and my best friend. You have been there from the beginning, at the very heart of this whole process—through the joys, the frustrations, the discouragements, and the celebrations. Thank you for journeying all of it with me. This book is a story of friendship, and I thank God every day for yours.

And to my family: Adam, thank you for challenging me always, for inspiring me to ask hard questions and to be a better version of myself. I'm proud to be your sister, and I hope I'm more like you when I grow up.

Dad, thank you for being the rock of our family, and for loving us so well. Thank you for your humor and your love and your never-ending encouragement. Thank you for showing me what it means to be faithful, honest, and kind.

And last, to my sweet Momma: no one could care more about this book than you have. Thank you for being my cheerleader, my confidant, my champion, and my friend. You raised me to be creative and helped me to believe I have a story to tell. It's only by your unconditional love that I've had the bravery to write this book. You will always be my forever editor.

Thank you, to each of you, for the impact you've had on my journey. I love you all.

I am because you are.

 *NOTES*

Chapter 1: On Seasons & Arriving

1. Oswald Chambers, "God's Purpose or Mine?" in *My Utmost for His Highest* (Nashville: Thomas Nelson, 1992), July 28 devotional.
2. Courtney E. Martin, *Perfect Girls, Starving Daughters: The Frightening New Normalcy of Hating Your Body* (New York: Free Press, 2007), 18.

Chapter 2: On Beauty & Seeing

1. Luke 12:48.

Chapter 3: On Time & Becoming

1. Margery Williams, *The Velveteen Rabbit* (New York: Avon, 1975), 13.
2. Madeleine L'Engle, *Walking on Water: Reflections on Faith and Art* (New York: North Point, 1980), 98.
3. Emily Dickinson, "Forever—is Composed of Nows—," in *The Poems of Emily Dickinson*, ed. R. W. Franklin (Cambridge, MA: Harvard University Press, 2005), 480.

Chapter 4: On Love & Choosing

1. Ralph Waldo Emerson, "Friendship," in *Emerson: Essays and Lectures* (New York: Library of America, 1983), 351.

Chapter 5: On Vocation & Beginning

1. "Fergie Undercover: The Duchess of York Bluffs Her Way into Orphanages in Turkey," Chris Rogers, *Daily Mail*, November 2,

2008, http://www.dailymail.co.uk/femail/article-1082355
/Fergie-undercover-The-Duchess-York-bluffs-way-orphanages
-Turkey.html.

2. Michael Hyatt, "What to Do When You Don't Know What
to Do: 3 Steps to Follow When You're Tired of Feeling
Uncertain," *Michael Hyatt* (blog), July 8, 2016, https://
michaelhyatt.com/what-to-do-when-you-dont-know-what
-to-do.html. Note: My mom read this quote in a newsletter
sent by Michael Hyatt, and now she says it all the time!

3. "William Wordsworth Quotes," BrainyQuote.com, August
21, 2016, http://www.brainyquote.com/quotes/quotes/w/
williamwor120835.html.

Chapter 6: On Injustice & Meaning

1. I first read about Frankl's philosophy in one of my friend, Don
Miller's email blasts from his company Storyline.

Chapter 7: On Fear & Walking

1. Maya Angelou, *I Know Why the Caged Bird Sings* (New York:
Random House, 2009).

2. "Mulberry Street May Fade, but 'Mulberry Street' Shines On,"
Michael Winerip, *New York Times*, January 29, 2012, http:
//college.usatoday.com/2015/09/21/controversial-1-in-5-sexual
-assault-statistic-validated-in-new-national-survey/.

Chapter 8: On Impact & Bearing

1. William Blake, "The Little Black Boy," in *Songs of Innocence and
Experience* (Princeton: Princeton University Press, 1994), 42.

Chapter 9: On Friendship & Missing

1. John Donne, *Devotions upon Emergent Occasions* (Oxford: Oxford
University Press, 1975), 198.

Chapter 10: On Wanderlust & Exploring

1. Quoted by Andy Warhol, AZQuotes, http://azquotes.com/
quote/481230.

2. Dr. Seuss, *Oh, the Places You'll Go!* (New York: Random House,
1990).

Chapter 11: On Desire & Serving

1. C. S. Lewis, *Mere Christianity* (New York: Harper One, 2015), 135.

2. "You can easily judge the character of a man by how he treats those who can do nothing for him." James D. Miles, as quoted in *Quotable Quotes* (New York: Penguin, 1997).

Chapter 12: On Wonder & Believing

1. Donald Miller, *Blue Like Jazz: Nonreligious Thoughts on Christian Spirituality* (Nashville: Thomas Nelson, 2003), 100.
2. Col. 1:16–17.

Chapter 13: On Style & Communicating

1. Maya Angelou in *The Arts Go to School: Classroom-Based Activities That Focus on Music, Painting, Drama, Movement, Media, and More*, David Booth and Masayuki Hachiya, eds. (Ontario: Pembroke Publishers, 2004), 14.
2. Lucy Maud Montgomery, *Anne of Green Gables* (New York: Grosset & Dunlap, 1908), 168.

Chapter 15: On Perfection & Failing

1. http://www.nytimes.com/2012/01/30/education/dr-seuss -book-mulberry-street-turns-75.html.

Chapter 16: On Dreams & Calling

1. Dan Pallotta, "The Way We Think about Charity Is Dead Wrong," TED video, 18:54, filmed March 2013, http: //www.ted.com/talks/dan_pallotta_the_way_we_think _about_charity_is_dead_wrong.
2. "Mind the Gaps," Deloitte 2015 Millenial Survey: Executive Summary, 2015, http://www2.deloitte.com/content/dam /Deloitte/global/Documents/About-Deloitte/gx-wef-2015 -millennial-survey-executivesummary.pdf.
3. Dan Eldon, *The Journey is the Destination: The Journals of Dan Eldon* (San Francisco: Chronicle Books, 2011).
4. Quoted in Linda Sargent Wood, *A More Perfect Union* (Oxford: Oxford University Press, 2010), 10.
5. Dave Lomas, *The Truest Thing about You: Identity, Desire, and Why It All Matters* (Colorado Springs: David C. Cook, 2014).

Chapter 18: On Journeys & Resting

1. William Shakespeare, *Macbeth*, act 2, scene 2, line 36.
2. Greg McKeown, "The Difference Between Successful and

Very Successful People," *Entrepreneur,* January 6, 2015, https: //www.entrepreneur.com/article/240878.

Chapter 20: On Pain & Surviving
1. Rom. 5:3–5.

Chapter 21: On Darkness & Healing
1. Anne Lamott, *Plan B: Further Thoughts on Faith* (New York: Riverhead, 2005), 66.
2. Julian of Norwich, *Revelations of Divine Love* (Brewster, MA: Paraclete Press, 2011), ix.